HUNTINGTON LIBRARY PUBLICATIONS

JAMES IRVINE, I
(1827-1886)

JAMES IRVINE, II
(1867-1947)

JAMES IRVINE, III
(1893-1935)

MYFORD IRVINE
(1898-1959)

THE
IRVINE RANCH

BY ROBERT GLASS CLELAND

Revised with an Epilogue by

ROBERT V. HINE

THE HUNTINGTON LIBRARY
San Marino, California

The publication of this volume has been
made possible by The James Irvine Foundation

Printed in the United States of America
by The Castle Press

Cover design by Ward Ritchie

TWENTY-TWO YEARS LATER

Rodman W. Paul

In the twenty-two years since Robert V. Hine edited the third edition of this little book, immense changes have swept over the lands that James Irvine and his associates acquired more than a century ago. Today the one-time sheep ranch is ambitiously promoting itself as a national, perhaps even international, center of high technology and bioscience. Big office buildings, large "industrial parks," hotels, shopping centers, a major university, an airport, and huge tracts of new homes, the latter mostly arranged in carefully planned "villages," dominate the rolling lands where once James Irvine's sheep were the only inhabitants. According to the Irvine Company, nearly 120,000 people live on the Irvine Ranch today and almost 150,000 have jobs there in the offices, industrial firms, and retail stores.

Behind these dramatic and visible alterations in the life of the huge property (the Ranch is still the largest private landowner in Orange County, even after selling thousands of acres) lie fundamental legal changes. Some fifty-two percent of the stock in the Irvine Company, which is a business enterprise, passed to the Irvine Foundation, a charitable trust established by James Irvine II in 1937. When new federal tax laws forced the Foundation to reduce its stock holdings in the company to not more than two percent, the latter company put itself up for sale and found a purchaser willing to pay $334,700,000. Subsequently, in 1983, a key member of the consortium putting up this massive sum, Donald L. Bren, bought out his partners by paying $517,-000,000 for the fifty-one percent of the stock that they then owned. Bren had been active for years as a vigorous leader in planning, developing, and building large-scale new communities in Orange County.

Under Bren's leadership the Irvine Company settled an issue that had caused friction for years, namely, the company's policy of leasing rather than selling its land to homeowners; built up local goodwill by electing Orange County business people to the board of directors; and launched upon the ambitious plans for high technology and bioscience already mentioned. Bren has continued and refined the policy of planned growth that has long distinguished the Irvine property from its sprawling neighbors. One of Bren's hopes, now in the design stage, is to build a center for technology, industry, and business that may ultimately employ 100,000 people. What an enormous change from sheep-ranch days!

San Marino, 1984

PREFACE
TO THE 1962 EDITION

Robert Glass Cleland was beloved and respected for so many qualities that to isolate one is an act of arrogance; nevertheless, if I were asked to nominate his prime professional excellence, I would single out the ability to see the general in the particular. Taking a small piece of land, as in his *Place Called Sespe*, or a single building, as in *El Molino Viejo*, or a business firm, as in *A History of Phelps Dodge*, Cleland had a remarkable knack of evoking from one story the whole development of a region. Thus for him, giving "a voice to the downs" (in that quotation from Wingfield-Stratford which he always loved) meant transforming antiquarian narrowness into a broader historical vision.

Nowhere did this particular genius of Robert Cleland better reveal itself than in his history of the Irvine Ranch. From Indian hut through Spanish conquest, Mexican rancho, and Anglo-American invasion to modern urbanization, he managed from a microcosm to project a narrative that illuminates all of southern California.

In editing Cleland's book for a new edition, a minimal amount of earlier, less relevant data, such as Indian custom, has been excluded to make room for the history of the ranch in the ten years since Cleland wrote. In gathering material for this recent period, I am deeply indebted to the following people: Mr. Charles S. Thomas, Mr. Arthur J. McFadden, Mr. N. Loyall McLaren, Mr. Charles S. Wheeler, III, Mr. William H. Spurgeon, III, Mr. Robert W. Long, and Mrs. Joan Irvine Burt, to mention only a few of the many at the Irvine Ranch who have given time and counsel; Mr. William L. Pereira and Mr. Jack Bevash, architects; Mr. Walter Burroughs, newspaper editor; and last, but in many ways first, Miss Mary Jane Bragg of the Huntington Library. To all, my sincerest thanks.

R. V. H.

Riverside, California
July 1, 1962

FOREWORD

The Irvine Ranch of Orange County is one of the few large land-holdings of southern California that have survived the vicissitudes and revolutionary changes of the passing generations. The ranch owed its origin to the old land-grant system of the Spanish-Mexican regime. It has now been in the possession of a single family for over eighty years and thus enjoys a continuity of ownership rare indeed in this particular portion of the state. It still retains substantially the area and boundaries established by its founder. Its written records, though not complete, are voluminous and accessible.

Such saving factors made it possible to write the present history. I have endeavored to give the book due measure of local color, embody in it some of the historical background of the region in which the ranch is located, and make the study an illuminating chapter in the agricultural and social evolution of southern California.

In gathering material for the volume, I have supplemented the Irvine Ranch letter books and records with newspaper files, official documents and records, personal interviews, and such secondary accounts as the extremely valuable volumes of the *Orange County History Series*. In the account of the Spanish-California era of the ranch, I have quoted freely from my social and economic history of early southern California, *The Cattle on a Thousand Hills*, and reprinted the Los Angeles *Star*'s lengthy account of the murder of Sheriff J. R. Barton which appeared in the Appendix of that volume.

Many people in many ways have given valuable assistance in the preparation of this account. Mr. John H. McCoy of Santa Ana first suggested that I write the volume. Mr. Myford Irvine . . . and Mr. W. B. Hellis . . . generously co-operated in answering many questions, supplying necessary data, and giving me free use of the ranch records.

Dr. Glenn Dumke of Occidental College rendered invaluable service in collecting and organizing a great body of research material. Dr. Frederick W. Hodge and Mr. Mark R. Harrington of the

Southwest Museum of Los Angeles generously reviewed my account of the early Indian inhabitants of the ranch. The resources of the Santa Ana Public Library, the Charles W. Bowers Memorial Museum of Santa Ana, and the Huntington Library of San Marino were freely placed at my disposal. I have imposed on Dr. Dumke, Dr. Edwin Carpenter, and Mr. W. W. Robinson, author and authority on California land titles, for whose counsels and suggestions I am especially indebted, to read the galley proof of the book. . . . To all of these, as well as to Mr. William McPherson of Santa Ana and to Mr. Carey S. Bliss and Miss Haydée Noya of the Huntington Library, I offer my sincere appreciation.

Above all, I am again under deep and lasting obligation to my secretary, Miss Norma Jones, and to my never-wearying, never-impatient friend, Dan S. Hammack.

Some years ago, in a Foreword to the history of another California ranch I quoted Wingfield-Stratford's striking sentence: "A knowledge of history is able to make the whole landscape alive, to render the exploration of the humblest village an adventure of thrilling possibilities, to give a voice to the downs and to enrich the waste with memories."

To the residents of Orange County, and all others who fall beneath the region's magic spell, I hope that this volume will make the smiling landscape more alive and enrich the fruitful land with memories.

The Huntington Library   ROBERT G. CLELAND
San Marino, California
1952

ix

CONTENTS

ILLUSTRATIONS

THE IRVINE RANCH

1

NATIVE AND SPANIARD

The Spaniards began the colonization of California with the establishment of a royal presidio at San Diego in July 1769. On the 14th of that month, "the day of the seraphic doctor San Buenaventura," Don Gaspar de Portolá, commander in chief of the expedition, and a company of trail-hardened friars, leather-jacket soldiers, muleteers, servants, and Indian neophytes left the infant settlement for the far-off, half-mythical port of Monterey.

Two weeks later, while encamped on the banks of a tree-lined stream, the company experienced four such "horrifying" earthquakes in a single day that it seemed appropriate to Father Juan Crespí, one of the friars of the expedition, to call the shallow watercourse the River of the Sweet Name of Jesus of the Earthquakes. Out of respect for St. Anne, the Mother of the Virgin, however, the hard-bitten soldiers, Crespí's companions, named the stream El Río de Santa Ana, and by that name the river is still known.

Rising in the high sierra above San Bernardino, the Santa Ana flows southward across the San Bernardino plain, follows the winding Santa Ana Cañon through the rough, chaparral-covered Santa Ana Mountains, enters the lower Santa Ana Valley at the small settlement of Olive, and finally reaches the sea slightly west of the city of Newport. During its hundred-mile-long course, Father Crespí's River of the Sweet Name of Jesus of the Earthquakes thus traverses parts of three southern California counties—San Bernardino, Riverside, and Orange.

The valley of the Santa Ana, between the Santa Ana Mountains and the sea, is one of the richest agricultural regions in California and the site of numerous prosperous towns and cities, including Anaheim, Santa Ana, Fullerton, and Orange. It is also the seat of the great landed estate known now for some ninety years as the Irvine Ranch.

Roughly oblong in shape (except for a large, curving segment along its northeastern border), the ranch is approximately twenty-two miles long by nine miles wide, once included well over a hundred thousand acres, and still covers over eighty-eight thousand. Its main axis runs northeast by southwest; its environs are remarkable for their striking contrasts.

On the northeast, for many miles, the ranch shares a common boundary line with the Cleveland National Forest, a region of lofty peaks and rough, brush-covered ranges. Its long northwestern boundary runs in part through mountainous, uncultivated land and in part through rich, highly productive plains. In the extreme southeast, the ranch is bordered by orchards, fields, and extensive grazing lands. From Newport to Laguna its southwestern boundary embraces crowded harbor, winding estuary, and bold, high cliffs that front upon the sea.

At the time of the Spanish occupation of California, there were approximately 250,000 Indians living in the province, a figure that represented about a fourth of the entire native population of what is now continental United States when

Columbus discovered the New World. The southern California coastal plain, including present-day Orange County, was one of the major centers of Indian population.

The natives of the region now included in the Irvine Ranch were Gabrielinos—that is, Indians of Shoshonean stock who occupied a large part of the Los Angeles plain and the San Gabriel and Santa Ana valleys. Traces of the Gabrielino culture have also been found on the channel islands of Santa Catalina and San Clemente.

In addition to many smaller settlements, the Gabrielinos had at least three major centers of population on or near the present Irvine Ranch. One, called Pahav, was located about fifteen miles southeast of Corona, just north of the Santa Ana Mountains and the ranch boundary. A second, Moyo, was situated north of the Newport Bay estuary; and a third, Lukup, occupied a site near the ocean, west of the mouth of the Santa Ana River.

According to Alfred L. Kroeber, a distinguished authority on the Indians of California, because the Gabrielinos held "the great bulk of the most fertile lowland portion of Southern California" and thus enjoyed a more abundant food supply and easier living conditions than their neighbors, they attained a higher cultural level than any other Indian group south of the Tehachapi and communicated elements of that culture to other villages.

The life that went on along the banks of Río Santa Ana before the Spaniards came was infinitely far removed from that which our own day is witness to. But the small, crude rancherias of the Gabrielinos, the myths, ceremonies and shadowy gods of a childlike race, the silence and solitude of an age-old wilderness are still part of the heritage of the Irvine Ranch.

The Spanish occupation of California, like that of all similar provinces of the Kingdom of New Spain, was carried out by means of three institutions designed especially for the settlement of the frontier, namely the presidio, the pueblo, and the mission. Though radically different both in character and purpose, these institutions had at least two things in common—all three were established to aid in the subjugation, control, and civilization of the frontier, and all three depended upon land grants from the crown for their existence.

Such royal grants were based upon an ancient principle of Spanish law that recognized the king as owner in fee simple of all the colonial possessions in the New World and vested in him private title to the fabulous resources of a continent. "We give, grant, and assign forever to you and to your heirs and successors, Kings of Castile and León," ran the famous bull of Alexander VI in 1493, "all and singular the aforesaid countries and islands thus unknown and hitherto discovered by your envoys and to be discovered hereafter, together with all their dominions, cities, camps, places, and towns as well as all rights, jurisdictions, and appurtenances of the same whereon they may be found."

It should be noted, however, that the royal grants to presidios and pueblos differed from the mission grants in two particulars: grants to presidios and pueblos were made in fee simple and included a fixed area of four square leagues, or about seventeen thousand acres; grants to the missions, on the contrary, though of enormous extent, were of a temporary nature and involved no transfer of title from the king.

So long as California was under Spanish rule, and indeed for a decade longer, the missions remained undisturbed in the use of their almost limitless landholdings. As the years went by, the ranges were covered with great herds of cattle, sheep, and horses, and thousands of Indian neophytes were brought under the teachings, discipline, and training of the friars. Meanwhile, however, a few royal grants, called ranchos, were bestowed on private individuals. The first of these were made in 1784 by Governor Pedro Fages to José María Verdugo, Juan José Domínguez, and Manuel Nieto, all of whom were members of the company of *soldados de cuero*, or "leather-jacket troops," that Fages had led to California in 1769.

The grant to José María Verdugo was named the Rancho San Rafael and included over thirty-six thousand acres between the Arroyo Seco, the Los Angeles River, and the La Cañada hills. Juan José Domínguez received sixteen square leagues, or approximately seventy-two thousand acres, running westward from the San Gabriel River to Redondo Bay and embracing all the territory now included in Palos Verdes, San Pedro, and Wilmington.

Manuel Nieto, to whom Governor Fages showed unusual generosity, was awarded a principality of nearly three hundred thousand acres. The San Gabriel River, which then emptied into the ocean near the present entrance to Long Beach harbor, formed the grant's western boundary; twenty-five miles down the coast the Santa Ana River marked its limits on the east; and from the lonely shore line of the Pacific his unfenced leagues of grazing lands spread away to the north to meet "the main road leading from San Diego along the hills to San Gabriel."

During the remainder of the Spanish regime and for the first ten or twelve years of Mexican rule, about thirty private rancho grants were made in all California; but in 1833 the Mexican government "secularized" the California missions, took over almost all of their immense landholdings, and distributed many millions of acres to Mexican citizens who applied for grants of government lands.

At the time of the American conquest of California in 1846, these large grants or ranchos were the dominant feature of the province's economic and social life. They remained the controlling factor in much of the state's settlement and agricultural development for many years, and their gradual conversion into cities, towns, and farming communities in large measure brought into being the southern California we know today. The ranchos thus constituted one of the few enduring legacies that California inherited from Mexico and Spain. Two such grants and part of a third went into the making of the Irvine Ranch.

2

MEXICAN GRANTS

In applying for a land grant under Mexican law, the petitioner asserted that he was a native-born or naturalized Mexican citizen; gave the location, boundaries, approximate size, and identifying landmarks of the desired tract; testified that none of the land in question had been included in a previous concession; declared that he was prepared to stock the holdings with the number of horses and cattle required by law; listed the names of the neighboring ranches; and supplied a *diseño*, or rough topographical map, of the property. The *diseño* showed not only the boundaries of the grant but also the hills, watercourses, marshes, wastelands, and other landmarks mentioned in the petition.

The procedure incident to the approval of a grant was as follows: "After examination by the governor, the petition and *diseño* were forwarded for verification to a local official of the district in which the land was located. If this official reported favorably on the concession, the governor gave his approval to the application, in set phraseology beginning, 'Complete what is commenced', and closing, 'Thus I command it, decree it, and sign it, which I certify.' He then ordered a formal grant, bearing his signature, to be given to the petitioner. A blotter copy, or *borrador*, was retained in the governor's office and a minute of the transaction was entered in a record book, called the *toma de razón*. The petition, *diseño*, and *borrador* were then assembled in a file called an *expediente* and placed in the provincial archives."[1] As a final step in the procedure the land was officially surveyed and juridical possession bestowed upon the owner.

The survey was carried out under the supervision of a magistrate, a number of "assisting witnesses," and the neighboring rancheros. The men who "filled the office of surveyor"—in other words, carried out the actual measurement—"made oath by God our Lord, and the sign of the Cross, to use it faithfully and legally to the best of their knowledge and understanding without deceit or fraud against any person."

Mounted on horseback, the two "surveyors" measured the boundaries of the grant, using for that purpose a rawhide cord, or *reata*, the ends of which were attached to long stakes. Upon the completion of the survey, in a ceremony closely resembling the rite that was followed by the conqueror or explorer who took possession of a new country in the name of the crown, the grantee "entered upon and walked over said lands, pulled up grass, scattered handfuls of earth, broke off branches of trees, and performed other acts and demonstrations of possession as signs of the possession which he said he took of said lands."

Surveys made under the conditions just outlined were at best only rough-and-ready makeshifts, and in later years their inaccuracies proved the source of endless controversy

[1]Robert G. Cleland, *The Cattle on a Thousand Hills* (San Marino, 1941), p. 34. A revised and enlarged edition of this work appeared in 1951.

and led to an immense amount of litigation. Corner posts on a grant were sometimes branded with the owner's iron, or cattle mark; but often the most convenient objects at hand—a steer's skull fixed in a bush, a clump of cactus, a few notches on a tree trunk, the place where two roads crossed, a mound at the entrance to a coyote's den, the edge of a dry barranca, a brush ramada on the banks of a stream, a spring of running water—were used to mark the boundary lines.

With the passage of the years, such landmarks usually disappeared or became almost impossible to locate and identify, thus adding another prolific source of confusion to the muddled state of California land titles. Even now, after the lapse of over a hundred years, the boundary lines of a few old Spanish-Mexican grants are occasionally before the courts for adjudication.

The validity of a grant depended upon the fulfillment of certain simple conditions, such as building a house, stocking the land with cattle, and planting a few fruit or shade trees along the boundary lines. If the stipulated requirements were not met, the grant could legally be annulled and the land thrown open again for denouncement or pre-emption. Instances of such forfeiture, however, were extremely rare.

One of the early Spanish grants in California—and for our purposes the most important—included a tract of approximately 62,516 acres that lay on the east bank of the Santa Ana River and extended from the Santa Ana Mountains to the sea.[2] The grant was called the Rancho Santiago de Santa Ana, sometimes abbreviated to Rancho Santiago.

---

[2]The grant was confirmed "for 11 square leagues," about 50,000 acres, but the phrase "containing 62,516 acres" was added.

As early as 1801, José Antonio Yorba, a Catalan volunteer in the Portolá expedition of 1769, and his father-in-law, Juan Pablo Grijalva, an Anza colonist of 1776, began to pasture their livestock on the land later included in this grant, without seeking formal permission from the governor for the privilege. Grijalva died in 1806. Three years later, Yorba addressed a communication to the provincial governor, Señor José Joaquín de Arrillaga, requesting confirmation of the grant, for which, he said, Grijalva had applied prior to his death. Freely translated, Yorba's petition, written by his son, Tomás, ran as follows:

Señor Governor: Antonio Yorba, a retired sergeant of the company of the Presidio of San Diego, herewith declares that while your Excellency was governor ad interim of Lower California the Ensign Don Pablo Grijalva, since deceased, presented a petition, by the hand of Don Manuel Rodríguez, requesting a grant of the place called "Santiago." On this rancho, the Ensign Don Pablo Grijalva and your petitioner, Antonio Yorba, proposed to build a house, cultivate the land, and graze their stock under a copartnership agreement.

I am aware that the said Grijalva made no mention of me or of my interest in the grant when he presented the aforesaid petition for the place called "Santiago," but the partnership agreement had been entered into as I have stated and the ranch remained under our joint ownership until Don Pablo's death.

Since that time, various people have been placed in charge of the affairs of the ranch but now Juan Peralta (my nephew) and I have agreed to a joint control of the property. One of my sons will represent my interests and we will stock the land with three hundred head of cattle and the same number of horses.

In view of the foregoing circumstances, I beg your Excellency to approve my petition for a confirmation of the grant. I beg your Excellency also to remember that I have a large family which, at the advanced age of sixty, I cannot support by my own labor.

Upon receipt of Yorba's request, the governor followed the procedure prescribed both by law and custom and ordered a local official, in this instance Lieutenant Francisco María Ruíz, to investigate the case. Failing to find Grijalva's original petition in the archives, Ruíz interviewed Grijalva's widow, Doña Dolores Valencia, regarding the matter. The latter said that she had seen the document (presumably bearing the governor's endorsement), but did not know what had happened to it. Under any condition, she had no objection to the recognition of Yorba and Peralta as the owners of the ranch. Governor Arrillaga accordingly approved Yorba's request, July 1, 1810, and ordered the uncle and nephew to be given possession of the land.

José Antonio Yorba died in 1825, leaving his half interest in the Rancho Santiago de Santa Ana, in undivided shares, to his widow and four sons.[3] Meanwhile, Mexico having attained independence, California had become a Mexican rather than a Spanish province. The change of sovereignty caused some concern among certain rancheros as to the validity of the land grants issued by the Spanish crown, and they petitioned the governor of California for a confirmation of the older titles. In 1839, Don José Antonio, eldest son of Don José Yorba, filed such a petition requesting the provincial government to confirm Governor Arrillaga's original grant of 1810.

In his petition to the governor, Don José declared that he had lived on the ranch for twenty-seven years, built three houses on it for himself and his children, pastured the land with cattle, horses, sheep, goats, and asses, planted a vine-

[3]A translation of Antonio Yorba's will, dated July 24, 1824, appears in the Orange County Historical Society, *Orange County History Series*, II (Santa Ana, Calif., 1932), 89-93.

yard and orchard, and each year raised various kinds of grain.

Adding, "I see myself at present with a numerous family," as further justification for his petition, Yorba assured the governor that he was trying, with tolerable success, to give his children a good education and that they in turn were assisting in the operation of the ranch. Some of the children were married; he had many grandchildren and needed to add greatly to his livestock to make proper provision for his rapidly increasing family.

Yorba's petition was submitted to the *ayuntamiento* or town council of Los Angeles, a body which then had jurisdiction in civil, criminal, and municipal matters "from the limits of San Juan Capistrano on the south to San Fernando on the north and eastward to the San Bernardino mountains . . . an area now comprised in four counties and . . . as large as the state of Massachusetts."

In September 1839, Juan C. Vejar and Januario Avila, who constituted the Committee on Vacant Lands of the *ayuntamiento*, reported that they had visited the Rancho Santiago de Santa Ana and found on it herds of horses and cattle as well as flocks of sheep and goats, two dwelling houses, crops of different kinds of grain, and a vineyard. All of these belonged to the petitioner, Don José Antonio Yorba, who had been in possession of the ranch for thirteen or fourteen years. The grant did not infringe on the rights of any other ranchero, and the committee therefore recommended that the *ayuntamiento* formally approve Yorba's petition.

This action was taken on September 25, 1839, and the prefect of the district so advised Don Manuel Jimeno Casarín, then acting governor of California, and recom-

mended the confirmation of the grant. Jimeno Casarín returned the recommendation with instructions to indicate
the boundaries of the grant more clearly on the map or
diseño and to furnish the names of the owners of the contiguous ranchos. The prefect referred the governor's instructions to the *ayuntamiento*, the *ayuntamiento* passed them on
to its Committee on Vacant Lands, the Committee on Vacant
Lands placed them in the hands of Don José, and in January
1840 the latter submitted a new *diseño* accompanied by a
notation so ambiguously worded that it seemed more likely
to add to, rather than clear up, the confusion of the boundaries. But the officials of that day apparently understood Don
José's curious phraseology, and on February 2, 1840, the
governor approved the amended petition for the Rancho
Santiago de Santa Ana.

For many years after the confirmation of the grant, the
ranch remained in possession of the Yorba and Peralta families, with the individual members of those families holding
the land as tenants-in-common—a form of ownership then
almost universal in California but one that eventually involved the succession, heirs, and title of nearly every ranch
in confusion, controversy, and litigation.

Don Tomás, brother of José, was a typical California
aristocrat of the rancho period. In his well-known *Life in
California*, Alfred Robinson described him as follows:

The proprietor, "Don Tomas Yorba," a tall, lean personage, dressed
in all the extravagance of his country's costume, received us at the
door of his house. . . . Upon his head he wore a black silk handkerchief, the four corners of which hung down his neck behind.
An embroidered shirt, a cravat of white jaconet tastefully tied, a
blue damask vest, short clothes of crimson velvet, a bright green
cloth jacket, with large silver buttons, and shoes of embroidered

deer skin, comprised his dress. I was afterwards informed by Don Manuel, that on some occasions, such as some particular feast day or festival, his entire display often exceeded in value a thousand dollars.

Don Tomás Yorba died in 1845. A translation of his will, a certified copy of which is in the Huntington Library, follows. But the document which appears below is not merely the testament of the head of the famous Yorba family, heir to the oldest land grant in Orange County, owner of what is now part of the Irvine Ranch; it is the testament of a vanished age, a vivid if unconscious portrayal of a never-to-be-recaptured way of life. This is the will that the dying Don Tomás indited:

In the name of the Holy Trinity, Father, Son, and the Holy Ghost, three distinct persons and one true God, Amen.—1st Clause. Know all who may read this my last will and testament: that I—Tomas Antonio Yorba, native born resident of this department of California, legitimate son of Antonio Yorba and Josefa Grijalva—being sick, but, by divine mercy, in the full enjoyment of my reason, memory and understanding, believing, as I firmly do, in all the mysteries of our holy Catholic faith, which faith is natural to me, since I have lived in it from my infancy and I declare that I want to live in it as a faithful Christian and true Catholic, trusting that, for this reason, his divine Majesty will have mercy on me and will pardon all my sins, through the mysteries of our Lord Jesus Christ and the intercession of his most Holy Mother, who is my protector and benefactress in these my last moments, so that together with my guardian angel, with St. Joseph, my own name's saint, and all the other saints of my devotion and all the other hosts of heaven, they will assist me before the grand tribunal of God, before which all mortals must render account of their actions—make and decree this my last will and testament as follows, on ordinary paper because of lack of stamped paper.—2nd Clause. Firstly, I commend my soul to God who created it, and my body to the earth, from whence it was fashioned, and it is my wish that I be buried in the shroud of our father St. Francis, the funeral to be according to what my executors and heirs consider that I deserve and is befitting.—3rd Clause. Item: in regard to the expense of the funeral and masses, these should be drawn from the fifth of my estate, according to the disposition of my executors, and I leave the residue of this fifth to my son Juan.—4th Clause. I declare that with respect to my debts, my heirs and executors should collect and pay any legal claims that may turn up or be due according to law. Item: I declare to have been married to Doña Vicenta Sepulveda, legitimate daughter of Don Francisco Sepulveda and Doña Ramona Serrano, of this neighborhood, by which marriage I have five children named: 1) Juan; 2) Guadalupe, deceased; 3) Jose Antonio; 4) Josefa; 5) Ramona. The first being 10 years old, the second died at the age of three, the third six years old, the fourth four years old and the fifth two years old. Item: I declare to have given my wife jewels of some value as a wedding present, but I do not remember how many, nor their value; but they must be in her possession, since I gave them to her.—Item: According to my reckoning I have about 2,000 head of cattle, 900 ewes and their corresponding males, three herds of about 100 mares and their stallions, and three donkeys; about 21 tame horses, 7 tame 12 unbroken mules; and lastly, whatever cattle, horses or mules may turn up with my brand which may not have been legally sold.—Item: I declare to have the right—through inheritance from my father—to part of middle Santa Ana and Lower Santa Ana, known to be of the Yorbas. I have in Middle Santa Ana an adobe house, its roof being part timber and part thatched, consisting of 18 rooms, including the soaphouse.—Item: I declare that I have two vineyards with wooden fences which are now planted with bearing vines and some fruit trees; also a section of enclosed land. . . .—6th Clause. I name as my heirs my children and my wife, in the form and manner indicated by the laws, following the necessary inventory. . . .

To which I, the citizen Vicente Sanchez, 1st constitutional Alcalde and Judge of the 1st *instancia* of the city of Los Angeles, certify; and I affirm that the present testamentary disposition was made in my presence, and that the testator, Don Tomas Antonio

Yorba, although ill, finds himself in the full command of his faculties and natural understanding, and, to attest it, I do this before the assistant witnesses—the citizens Ramon Aguilar and Ignacio Coronel—the other instrumental witnesses being the citizens Bautista Mutriel and Mariano Martinez; on the 28th day of the month of January, 1845. The testator did not sign because of physical inability, but Don Juan Bandini signed for him. . . .

[Signed] Vicente Sanchez

Ignacio Coronel   Jacob Frankfort[4]

After the death of Don Tomás, the Rancho Santiago de Santa Ana continued in possession of the Yorba and Peralta families for something over twenty years. But deaths, marriages, and the birth of numerous children and grandchildren made radical changes in the number and personnel of the tenants-in-common of the ranch and complicated still further the already greatly involved question of individual shares and individual rights.

Sometime after the mid-forties, Leandro Serrano, husband of Presentación Yorba, united the claims of the Peralta heirs with his wife's interest in the property and assumed control of the ranch. Serrano was married twice and had six children by one wife and seven by the other. He died in 1852, leaving to his numerous heirs a number of other large ranchos as well as his interest in the Santiago de Santa Ana.

By that time the claims of the many Yorbas, Peraltas, and Serranos to the sixty-one-thousand-acre property were hopelessly intertangled and confused. The situation was only slightly relieved when the Yorba heirs agreed to surrender all claim to the Peralta share of the Rancho Santiago de Santa Ana in return for a tract of land, slightly over a league in extent, in the lower Santa Ana Valley, which the Peralta family owned.

[4]Translation by Miss Haydée Noya of the Huntington Library.

Don Bernardo, patriarchal head of the large and influential Yorba family at the time of California's annexation by the United States, was one of the most distinguished figures of the romantic rancho era. His "home place" was the Rancho Cañon de Santa Ana, north of and just across the river from the Rancho Santiago de Santa Ana, and there he lived in much the style and fashion of the lord of a medieval manor. "By 1850," wrote Don Meadows,

the Hacienda de Las Yorbas was the social and business center of the Santa Ana Valley. The master's house became a two story structure of about thirty rooms, not including the school, harness shop, shoemaker's room, and other places occupied by dependents. In all there were more than fifty rooms arranged about a court or patio in the rear of the main residence. . . .

According to a descendant of Bernardo Yorba, the tradesmen and people employed about the house were: Four wool-combers, two tanners, one butter and cheeseman who directed every day the milking of from fifty to sixty cows, one harness maker, two shoemakers, one jeweler, one plasterer, one carpenter, one major-domo, two errand boys, one sheep herder, one cook, one baker, two washerwomen, one woman to iron, four sewing women, one dressmaker, two gardeners, a schoolmaster, and man to make the wine. . . . More than a hundred lesser employees were maintained on the ranch. The Indian peons lived in a little village of their own. . . .

The rancho had two orchards where various types of fruit were grown, and some wheat was raised. . . . Ten steers a month were slaughtered to supply the hacienda.

Don Bernardo was married three times and begat a total of sixteen children. When he died he was one of the three or four wealthiest rancheros in southern California and left an estate consisting of some thirty-seven thousand acres of land and other assets said to be worth over a hundred thousand dollars.

3

RANCHOS

The second of the three large land grants that later went wholly or in part into the making of the Irvine Ranch was known as the San Joaquin. This rancho consisted of two separate parcels—a tract sometimes called the Cerrito de las Ranas or Hill of the Frogs, and sometimes the Ciénega de las Ranas or Marsh of the Frogs, and an adjacent area known as La Bolsa de San Joaquin. The history of the two grants and their final merger into a single property, the Rancho San Joaquin, is worth a brief review.

One of the turning points in early California history, as previously indicated, was the so-called Secularization Act of 1833 under which the Mexican government repossessed and eventually distributed to private claimants all but a small fraction of the land that the Spanish crown had previously allocated to the California missions. At the time of the passage of this act, the Mission San Juan Capistrano had control of several hundred square miles of grazing lands, divided into a number of separate administrative units or ranchos.

One of these mission ranchos was the eleven-square-league Cerrito or Ciénega de las Ranas that adjoined the Santiago de Santa Ana on the southeast, extended from a familiar landmark, the Hill of the Frogs, in a southwesterly direction to the sea, and ran along the coast from what is now the city of Newport to Laguna Beach. The following passage explains in more detail the origin and various applications of the name. "A wide slough covered with tules ran back from the head of Newport Bay nearly to the foothills near Red Hill," wrote Terry E. Stephenson in 1931. "This slough was known to the Spaniards and Californians as Cienega de las Ranas, the Swamp of the Frogs. The proximity of Red Hill to the slough caused the hill to be called Cerrito de las Ranas, the Hill of the Frogs, generally on old maps spelled Serrito de las Ranas, and sometimes merely as Ranas. A spring of water near there was called Aguaje de las Ranas, and the canyon that is located back of Lemon Heights, reaching from the Irvine ranch house almost to the County Park, was called Canada de las Ranas."

José Andrés Sepúlveda, son of Francisco Sepúlveda, owner of the Rancho San Vicente, applied for a grant to the Cerrito de las Ranas in 1836, but the "Political Chief Magistrate, Don Nicolás Gutiérrez" failed to make the necessary report on the petition, and after about a year Sepúlveda carried the matter to the governor, Don Juan B. Alvarado.

Alvarado immediately sent the petition to the *ayuntamiento* of Los Angeles, and the latter appointed a committee to make the usual investigation and recommendations. The committee, in turn, acted with unusual dispatch. It reported that the petitioner, Don José Sepúlveda, was living with his father, that the latter's ranch was too small to support the combined herds of the two men, and that Don José had failed to receive official approval of the grant only because the California government was demoralized by factional strife and revolution.

The committee's report further pointed out that while the grant in question lay within the boundaries of land once occupied by the Mission San Juan Capistrano, the mission no longer had enough cattle to pasture either the Cerrito de las Ranas or a number of other ranchos to which it laid claim. The committee also found that Tomás Yorba, Sepúlveda's only rival for the grant, likewise had more land than he required for his stock. Upon the committee's recommendation, the *ayuntamiento* accordingly approved Sepúlveda's petition, and on April 15, 1837, Governor Alvarado confirmed the grant.

Four years later, Sepúlveda became engaged in an acrimonious boundary dispute with the father president of San Juan Capistrano. The friar claimed that Don José had willfully ignored the boundary limits established in the previous grant and taken possession of a large additional body of mission land.

Sepúlveda countered with a petition to the governor asking for a settlement of the dispute in his favor on the ground that the area of his grant had been extended beyond its original boundaries by Luís Arenas, alcalde of the pueblo of Los Angeles, to include the tract known as the Bolsa de San Joaquin, and that his cattle were using this supplemental land by virtue of the alcalde's action.

Prefect Santiago de Argüello, to whom Sepúlveda's petition was sent, found that the controversy would lead him into pretty deep waters and passed the matter back to Governor Alvarado for decision. In his report on the affair, however, Argüello pointed out that Arenas had no legal right to increase the size of the original grant, that Sepúlveda was thoroughly aware of this but hoped to obtain the land more or less by default if he said nothing about the alcalde's lack of authority, and that Don José's shady maneuver failed of its purpose only because the "Father Minister" of San Juan undertook to defend the rights of the mission.

For the time being, at least, Governor Alvarado agreed with Argüello's conclusions and wrote that while Sepúlveda was entitled to the grant of the Ciénega de las Ranas he could not go beyond the boundaries specified in the original grant. Argüello was accordingly instructed to settle the controversy between Don José and the mission on that basis.

Far from acquiescing in the governor's decision, however, Sepúlveda next filed a petition for a formal grant to the Rancho Bolsa de San Joaquin. Alvarado, following the prescribed practice, thereupon notified the prefect to investigate this new request of the resourceful Don José. Argüello obeyed instructions, but his report was adverse, detailed, and indignant. In substance he said:

First, that the petitioner was a slippery and dishonest person who persistently and willfully sought to mislead the lawful authorities; second, that Don José's petition represented the proposed grant as being four leagues square—a league shorter than the Bolsa's true length—and that the *diseño* or map accompanying the petition was drawn on such a distorted scale as to make the ranch appear only about a tenth as large as it really was; third, that Don Santiago Johnson and Don Juan Forster had formally solicited the grant and filed the required map of the property with the governor before Sepúlveda drafted his request; fourth, that Sepúlveda, far from obeying the governor's orders and keeping within the boundaries of his original grant, as he had been told to do, had deliberately "extended himself as far as the Eye can reach" and expanded the boundaries of his holdings "from one extremity to the other, unto the beach in the southerly direction and unto the mountains in the North"; and fifth, that the grant, as shown, even on Don José's own map, included sixteen square leagues, or five leagues more than the maximum area that the law of the Republic allowed in any one grant.

On these grounds, Argüello concluded, he strongly believed that Señor Sepúlveda's petition for the Bolsa de San Joaquin should be denied and that he should be strictly limited to the original grant of the Rancho Ciénega de las Ranas. The matter, however, was one which his Excellency, the Governor, and his "Superior Will," alone could decide.

Despite Argüello's apparently well-founded objections and his own previous suspicions of Sepúlveda's methods, on May 13, 1842, Alvarado approved Don José's petition for the Bolsa de San Joaquin and at once ordered the grant to be officially confirmed.

In accordance with the law and custom of the time, notice was given to the neighboring rancheros that the survey of the new grant would be made at such and such a time and that formal possession of the ranch would be given to Don José immediately thereafter unless legitimate protest were made. The Yorbas alone appeared to oppose the grant, but their objections were overruled, and Don José was given possession of the Bolsa de San Joaquin, a place that J. J. Warner described in the fifties as "a hummock, a kind of an Island, surrounded by a marsh."

Sepúlveda's two grants, the Ciénega de las Ranas and the Bolsa de San Joaquin, were apparently administered as a unit and soon became known as the Rancho San Joaquin. Here Don José built a large adobe house for himself and his family, converted a considerable acreage into fields and gardens, and grazed large herds of horses and cattle on his many unfenced leagues of rolling hills and far-reaching plains.

The third grant that entered into the making of the historic Irvine Ranch bore the engaging name of El Rancho Lomas de Santiago, or the Ranch of the Hills of St. James. As early as 1836 or 1837, Teodosio Yorba, a younger brother of the more famous Don Bernardo, pastured several thousand head of cattle on the site later included in this grant, constructed a number of irrigation ditches or canals, built a substantial corral, and erected a house in the Cañada de Santiago near the "old road to San Diego." The house, though nearly thirty feet long and perhaps twenty feet wide, was little more than a framework of wood covered with tule mats.

Don Teodosio lived on the ranch for nearly a decade without bothering to complete the formalities necessary for a valid title; but by 1846 it was apparent that the United States intended to annex California, and some of the more farsighted rancheros took steps to make their titles conform as far as possible to the previously ignored technical requirements of Mexican law. The owner of the Lomas de Santiago was one of this foresighted number.

Pío Pico, the governor of the province, was seeking to anticipate American annexation by making wholesale land grants to his friends and relatives, and even to himself, and Don Teodosio had no difficulty in getting that obliging official to authorize the necessary survey and formally invest him with the title by the ancient and picturesque rite of the act of possession.

Yorba's petition for the place of the Hills of St. James was approved on May 26, 1846, and the survey was made in July. The starting point of the latter was at Red Hill. The grant was bounded by the ranchos Santiago, San Joaquin, and El Toro (or Los Alisos) and the Cañada de Santiago.[1] It contained only four square leagues, more or less, and did not extend beyond Santiago Creek or Cañon. Because of curious happenings later on, it is well to keep both the original size and boundaries of this grant in mind.

Under normal conditions, the three grants—Santiago de Santa Ana, San Joaquin, and Lomas de Santiago—would have remained in the peaceful possession of many generations of the Yorba, Peralta, and Sepúlveda families. But even before the picturesque ceremony incident to the award of the last of the three grants was carried out, the twilight of the California of the Spanish-Mexican era—the California of mission, pueblo, and presidio, of ranchos and rancheros, of prodigal land grants and patriarchal families, of leisurely, carefree life and simple pastoral economy—had begun to fall.

Cota's certification of Don Teodosio's title to the Lomas de Santiago began, "In the City of Los Angeles, Capital of the Department of California, on the 7th day of July, 1846." On the same day, the 7th of July, 1846, the commander of a small fleet which lay at anchor in Monterey Bay disembarked a force of some two hundred and fifty men, seized the unresisting town, raised the American flag, fired a salute, and formally proclaimed the annexation of California to the United States.

Everything in California, including the ancient land grants and their recipients, was irrevocably altered by that event.

---

[1]Leonardo Cota, one of the alcaldes of Los Angeles, supervised the survey, traveling by horseback and pack train to the distant Santa Ana. Ygnacio Palomares, grantee of the ranchos Azusa and San José, and Juan Forster, Pico's brother-in-law, were his assistants.

4

AMERICANIZATION

At the time of the American conquest of California in 1846, as previously explained, all but a small remnant of the once vast mission holdings and large additional areas of the public domain were in the hands of private owners, and the rancho system dominated every phase of provincial life.

The Californians viewed the coming of the Americans with mixed feelings: some accepted it as the only way by which the province could be saved from anarchy, others feared that the American government would confiscate the existing land grants and otherwise penalize the native population.

Under the Treaty of Guadalupe Hidalgo, however, the United States government bound itself to protect the native Californians in the free enjoyment of their liberty, property, and religion and to give recognition to "legitimate titles to every description of property, personal and real, existing in the ceded territories."

In making this pledge to the Californians, the United States acted in honesty and good faith, but because of the social and economic bedlam created by the Gold Rush, a complex situation developed in California which Congress, far off and ill informed, did not fully appreciate or adequately meet.

The question of land ownership in California offered the American government a particularly difficult and involved problem. Owing to lost or defective documents, haphazard surveys, poorly defined boundaries, and unsatisfied requirements, the titles to many grants were technically imperfect and legally subject to forfeiture, even under Mexican law. The grants, too, were of many kinds and descriptions. Among them were "mission lands, pueblo lands, private lands, and public lands; titles technically complete and titles technically faulty; titles granted in good faith and titles granted solely to anticipate American annexation; titles free from any shadow of suspicion and titles obtained through obvious fraud."

Unfortunately, the exigencies created by the Gold Rush would not permit the land problem to work itself out in a gradual, normal, and orderly fashion but compelled the federal government to take hasty and ill-considered action to settle the complicated issues, in some fashion at least, before they overwhelmed the state.

On March 3, 1851, Congress passed a bill sponsored by William M. Gwin, one of the newly appointed senators from California and professed champion of the settlers' cause, that provided for a board of three "commissioners to ascertain and settle the private land claims in California." Under penalty of forfeiture, all California titles held under Spanish or Mexican grants were to be submitted to this board for adjudication within two years, but the decision of the board could be appealed either by the claimant or the government to the federal courts.

The board was formally organized in San Francisco on

December 8, 1851, and began regular hearings approximately two months later. During the next five years it considered over eight hundred cases, involving title to approximately twelve million acres, approved over five hundred claims, and rejected about half as many as it approved. The remaining claims were either dismissed by the commissioners or withdrawn by the petitioners.

Despite occasional charges of bias, sometimes by landholders, sometimes by settlers, the commissioners apparently performed their difficult and involved task as honestly and expeditiously as circumstances would permit. In nearly every instance, appeal was taken either by government or claimant from the board's decisions to the courts; but in seventy-five or eighty per cent of these cases the decrees of the commissioners were sustained.

Compliance with the procedure prescribed by the board for presentation of a claim and the assembling of documentary and other forms of proof necessary to validate a title put the landowners, especially those living in southern California, to enormous trouble and expense and placed the Spanish-Californians especially at serious disadvantage.

"Strangers to American laws and legal procedure, ignorant even of the language, they [the inhabitants of the land] were required to submit to judicial processes in which they were wholly inexperienced, and to defend their rights under proceedings they could not understand. The validity of many titles rested upon documents long since destroyed or forgotten, or upon the claimant's ability to produce eyewitnesses to events which had happened, in some cases, years before he himself was born. Land grants held time out of mind by succeeding members of the same family were attacked on the ground of technical imperfections, and boundaries recognized by custom and tradition for a generation were challenged by the government's attorneys."[1]

In the face of such conditions, the validation of even the most perfect title presented serious difficulties, frequently involved ruinous expense, and often entailed years of uncertainty and delay. In many instances legitimate costs were greatly magnified by the imposition of lawyers' excessive fees and other exorbitant charges. Lack of ready money—a characteristic feature of California's economic life throughout the colonial era—compelled most grant owners to sacrifice land and livestock to meet the costs of defending their titles, or to resort to the much more hazardous expedient of borrowing money to serve the same purpose.

To the native landowners, the pledge of the American government in the Treaty of Guadalupe Hidalgo to recognize "legitimate titles to every description of property . . . in the ceded territories," thus proved a bitter and costly delusion; and the fact that the clause was written into the treaty in good faith offered little consolation to the California ranchero whose property was stripped from him by the operation of the Act of 1851.

According to the economic historian John S. Hittell, one out of every ten of the bona fide landowners of Los Angeles County was reduced to bankruptcy by the federal land policy, and at least forty per cent of the land legitimately owned under Mexican grants was alienated to meet the costs of complying with the conditions prescribed by Congress. "The long lists of Sheriffs and mortgage sales in our newspapers," wrote Abel Stearns to John C. Frémont, "the depopulation of flourishing stock Ranches, and

---

[1]Cleland, *The Cattle on a Thousand Hills*, pp. 56-57.

the pauperism of Rancheros, but a short time since wealthy, all attest to disastrous consequences of too much litigation and of this unsettled state of titles."

In compliance with the Act of 1851 and the instructions issued by the land commissioners, Bernardo Yorba, Teodosio Yorba, and Ramón Yorba, heirs of Antonio Yorba and Juan Peralta, petitioned the Board of Land Commissioners for validation of their claim to the Rancho Santiago de Santa Ana. The petition was presented on November 9, 1852, by J. Lancaster Brent, one of the best-known southern California attorneys of that day, on behalf of the Yorba and Peralta heirs.

The petition was supported by numerous documents (some of which went back to the original Arrillaga grant of 1810), and by the testimony of such well-known Californians as Francisco Sepúlveda, Antonio F. Coronel, Santiago Argüello, José María Covarrubias, J. J. Warner, and José Desiderio Ybarra. The testimony of Ybarra was typical of the statements made by all the others:

My name is Desiderio Ybarra. My age is sixty nine years and I reside in Los Angeles.

I knew Antonio Yorba and Juan Peralta. They lived on the Rancho Santa Ana about twelve leagues from this place, in an Easterly direction. My father was in the employ of said Yorba and Peralta and established the Rancho for them in 1812 and they and their descendants have occupied it ever since. They had a house there in which they lived, they had a vineyard and orchard and cultivated the Land and had Cattle and other Stock there.

Juan Peralta died about Eighteen years ago. Antonio Yorba died many years ago, and before Peralta's death. They continued in the possession of the Rancho so long as they lived. They occupied separate houses on the Rancho. I knew the boundaries of the Rancho. They were Cerrito de las Ranas passing through the middle of the

"Cienega la Bolsa de Jengara[?]" to the Sea Coast, from the Sea Coast to the Santa Ana River and through the "levrito de Santiago" where it descends to the River.

There was a new *Channell* formed by the River Santa Ana by a flood of 1811. Previous to that the River flowed in its bed. Previous to the flood of 1811 Yorba & Peralta had a Cabin or small hut there which was destroyed by the freshet.

On July 10, 1855, nearly three years after the Yorba-Peralta petition was presented, the Land Commission approved the grant of the Rancho Santiago de Santa Ana, and the secretary of the board accompanied the notice of such action with the statement that the title to the rancho was both very old and very meritorious.

Following its invariable custom in such cases, however, the government appealed the decision of the Land Commission to the United States District Court. But the Yorba-Peralta title was without material flaws, and in 1857 the court dismissed the government's appeal and validated the grant.

The settlement of the legality of title, however, marked the beginning rather than the end of litigation over the involved question of the ownership of the half-century-old ranch.

Originally held by two kinsmen in equal shares, the huge ranch now counted its owners literally by the score, for California marriages were notably fecund; and with the coming of the third generation, the Yorba and Peralta heirs were no longer a simple family but a large, complicated clan.

Since scores of the heirs held undivided interests, great or small, in the grant, time inevitably brought conflict of interests, confusion of title, and ultimate breakup of the property. To make matters worse, a large number of the old tenant-in-common interests had passed into hands of outsiders so that the ranch was no longer the exclusive possession of the two families.

A few examples of the many sales and conveyances in which the individual Santiago de Santa Ana holdings were involved before the final partition of the great ranch will indicate the nature of the transactions themselves and show how seriously they complicated claims of ownership and title to the property.

As early as 1849, José del Carmen Lugo, alcalde of Los Angeles, ordered a partition of the Santiago de Santa Ana; but there were many irregularities in the proceedings, and the United States Land Commission subsequently voided the alcalde's action. Many sales and resales of individual claims were nevertheless made under Lugo's order, at prices so low as to seem today fantastically unreal.

In 1853, for example, Isabel Yorba transferred her undivided portion of the ranch to Teodosio Yorba for $200; the same year Guadalupe Yorba de Orozco sold her interest for $150; Ramón Yorba transferred his own and his sister's rights to Antonio F. Coronel for $1,500; Susana Yorba parted with her share for $100; in 1854 José Sepúlveda paid Domingo Yorba, one of the largest of the claimants, $6,000 in cash, a hundred heifers, fifty steers, and fifty fillies for his share of land and livestock.

Though one of the purchasers referred to in the preceding paragraph technically bought an undivided interest in the ranch, he actually negotiated for a particular tract of land and received what passed for a deed to the property in question. Domingo Yorba and his wife thus conveyed to José Sepúlveda "the land of the Rancho Santa Ana where they [the grantees] at present live to where the River of the said Rancho of Santa Ana runs, including all the houses, corrals, and fences to them belonging." José Ramón Yorba likewise deeded to Abel Stearns a small but specific portion of the ranch of which he held possession. The boundaries of the tract were defined in the following detail: "Commencing at the corner of the foot path separating the herein described premises from the garden of Teodosio Yorba and a certain road which separates these premises from the hills on the East; thence Northerly along the old fence as far as the lands of Desiderio Burruel; thence Westerly along the line of said Burruel marked by an old fence as far as the lands of the minor children of Tomás Yorba; thence Southerly along the lands of said children marked by an old fence to the above mentioned foot path; thence Easterly along said foot path and the garden of Teodosio Yorba to the point of beginning."

By a later deed, important especially because of the water rights involved, Desiderio Burruel and María Yorba, his wife, conveyed to Ramón Peralta a tract of land three hundred and fifty yards square, situated "in a hollow at one end of the farming land of the party of the first part, bounded East by the Camino del Refugio; North by the Road to Anaheim, and the lands of Doña Vicenta de Carrillo; South by the plain; West by the farming lands of the party of the first part. . . . The first party also agrees to give to the second party the right to use the water that he, the first party, has in possession. When it has performed its functions in the irrigation of his lands, the second party shall have the privilege to take it, he helping to keep the zanjas clean when in his possession."

Bernardo Yorba died in 1858, leaving more than twenty

children, at least half of whom were married, to inherit his interests in the Rancho Santiago de Santa Ana.

Like every other great ranch in southern California, the Santiago de Santa Ana, together with its owners and inhabitants, felt the effects of the Great Drought of the mid-sixties. Early in the drought the Yorbas sent some 3,000 head of cattle to their ranchos in Lower California, but presumably the greater part of the family's large herds eventually perished for lack of grass and water.

In the meantime, the number of Americans who held fractional interests in the ranch rapidly increased. By the mid-sixties the list of these "alien" owners included Felix Bachman, who at one time had the largest store in Los Angeles and played an important role in opening the trade between Los Angeles and Salt Lake; Frederick W. Koll, who lived in Los Angeles in the midst of an orange grove on what is now the southeast corner of Spring and Seventh streets; William Wolfskill, described in a later chapter; Ezra Drown, a well-to-do lawyer; Thomas D. Mott, whose wife, Ascención, was the daughter of Don José Andrés Sepúlveda, owner of the Rancho San Joaquin; Sam Brannan, who came to California as the leader of a Mormon colony, rose to fame and temporary fortune, and died in Escondido many years later, an impoverished and forgotten victim of drink and dissipation; Ben Holladay, the shrewd, domineering "Napoleon of the West," who made himself master of thirty-three hundred miles of stage lines between the Mississippi River and the coast; Isaias W. Hellman, founder of the Farmers and Merchants Bank of Los Angeles; and Abel Stearns, merchant, landowner, and ranchero, who more than any other man of his generation "personified both the southern California of the Mexican tradition and the southern California of the American period."[2]

Generally looked upon as the largest land and cattle owner in southern California in the early sixties, Stearns was hard hit by the drought, lost his far-famed Rancho Los Alamitos, and barely escaped a complete financial debacle. Various creditors, including the State of California and the well-known New York mercantile firm of Phelps, Dodge & Co. (which had advanced substantial sums for the development of Stearns's widely talked-of though wholly unprofitable tin mine at Temescal), issued attachments right and left upon his cattle, horses, and ranchos including his holdings in the Santiago; and for a time his great land and cattle empire seemed ready to disintegrate.

But after several doubtful years, Stearns weathered the crisis and in 1866 took the initiative in bringing suit for a division and distribution of the Rancho Santiago. The suit was directed against Leonardo Cota, husband of Inés Yorba de Cota and one of the largest owners of the ranch, and some sixty other defendants. In addition to Stearns, the plaintiffs in the case included various Yorbas, Peraltas, and Sepúlvedas, a number of older American residents of southern California, and certain recent arrivals from the northern part of the state who had previously bought William Wolfskill's interests in the ranch.

The names of the new claimants from the north were soon to become widely known throughout southern California. They were James Irvine, Benjamin and Thomas Flint, and Llewellyn Bixby.

[2]In addition to these Americans who from time to time, in one way or another, acquired an interest in the Santiago de Santa Ana, several well-known Californians, including Agustín Olvera, Antonio F. Coronel, Pacífico Ontiveras, Desiderio Burruel, Cristóbal Águilar, and Leonardo Cota, also obtained shares in the property.

The case of Abel Stearns et al. *v.* Leonardo Cota et al. was brought before Judge Pablo de la Guerra in the District Court of Los Angeles County in August 1866, and on February 24, 1868, de la Guerra rendered judgment in favor of the plaintiffs.

In his decision the court declared that "the tract of land anciently called 'Santiago' but also known as the 'Santiago de Santa Ana' and the 'Rancho de Santa Ana,'" contained 62,516 and a fraction acres and was held by its owners as tenants-in-common. He then gave a long list of these owners and the share of the ranch to which each was entitled.

Three referees or commissioners—S. D. Gavitt, James H. Sander, and J. J. Warner—were appointed to divide the property among the claimants as equitably as possible, taking into account the quality of the land, advantages of location, availability for cultivation, and any other circumstance or factor that might affect its value.

In spite of delay caused by bad roads and stormy weather, the commissioners finished their complicated task in a little over six months, and Judge de la Guerra accepted their report and recommendations and entered his final decree, including an item of over ten thousand dollars for costs and expenses assessed against the owners of the ranch, on September 12, 1868. The combined holdings of Irvine, Bixby, and the two Flints in the Rancho Santiago de Santa Ana came to approximately 3,800 acres. In the partition of the ranch, the commissioners assigned Irvine and his associates a strip of land, three quarters of a mile wide, that ran along the southeastern boundary of the ranch from its northern limits to the sea, a distance of approximately eight miles.

5

SEPÚLVEDA AND YORBA

Title to the San Joaquin, one of the two great Mexican grants that was later included in its entirety in the Irvine Ranch, was not affected by the complications and confusion in which the claims of scores of tenants-in-common and endless transfers of fractional interests involved the title of the Rancho Santiago de Santa Ana. But the owner of the San Joaquin did not escape the plague of debt and destructive interest charges that afflicted southern California like a financial Black Death during the fifties and sixties and left poverty and ruin in its path.

It has been said of Don José Andrés Sepúlveda, one of the most picturesque figures of the post–Gold Rush era, and owner of the two grants that made up the Rancho San Joaquin, that he "won romantic distinction for his great landholdings, fast race horses, reckless wagers, openhanded hospitality, and the elegance of his costumes."

Long before California's change of sovereignty, Sepúlveda had become famous—or notorious—for his love of horse racing and the prodigality of his wagers. His passion and audacity increased with the coming of the Americans. Probably his crowning achievement was the defeat of his chief rival, Pío Pico, in the most famous race in early California history.

In 1846, when Pío Pico's governorship and the Mexican regime came to a simultaneous end in California, the two brothers, Pío and Andrés, were among the three or four largest landowners in the state. Like Sepúlveda, they were also passionately devoted to horse racing and indulged quite as freely as Don José in the reckless wagers of the time.

During the latter part of 1851, Pío Pico offered to race his horse Sarco against any horse in the state for a distance of nine miles. Learning that an Australian-bred mare named Black Swan had won a number of races in northern California in record time, Sepúlveda arranged with the owners to bring the mare south to meet Pico's challenge.

The race took place in Los Angeles in March 1852. The starting point was about where Seventh Street now crosses Alameda, and the course ran along the latter street to a stake four and a half miles distant and back again to the starting point. According to Thomas D. Mott, one of the spectators of the race:

No preparations were made to put the track in condition, and not much of the race outside of start and finish was seen, as mustard on both sides of the road was ten feet high.

The length of the course was nine miles, or more properly speaking, three Spanish leagues. . . . Everybody in the country was present and the whole country as far north as San Luis Obispo and south to San Diego was depopulated. They all came to see the great race.

The wagers included "twenty-five thousand dollars in cash, . . . five hundred horses, five hundred mares, five hundred heifers, five hundred calves, and five hundred sheep." To the great chagrin and impoverishment of the Picos and the many other backers of the stallion, the mare won the race by some seventy-five yards.

After the victory, Sepúlveda bought Black Swan and took her back to the Rancho San Joaquin. There the mare stepped on a nail, contracted lockjaw, and died.

Some years ago, the late Terry E. Stephenson of Santa Ana, profound lover and foremost interpreter of the history of Orange County, unearthed an interesting court record giving the typical terms and conditions that governed the races of that time. The document related to a race backed by José and Fernando Sepúlveda and their perennial rivals, Pío and Andrés Pico, of the nearby Rancho Santa Margarita. Translated for the court from the ungrammatical Spanish in which it was originally written, the paper read as follows:

Today the 12th of October, 1852, we, José Sepúlveda and Pío Pico, the first in the name of his brother, Fernando Sepúlveda, and the second in the name of his brother, Andrés Pico, empowered by the parties, have determined to adjust and contract the following agreement:

First, José Sepúlveda is bound in the name of his brother, Fernando, to run on the 20th inst. a roan horse which ran with the Martilla horse, and the distance of the race shall be 450 varas.

Second, Pío Pico is bound in the name of his brother, Andrés, to run the race aforesaid with a sorrel horse of Santa Barbara which belongs to the Messrs. Ruices.

Third, this race shall be sported, staking on the issue, each party $1600 and 300 head of cattle, 200 of three years and upwards and 100 of one year and upwards. These cattle shall not be bulls, but steers and cows.

Fourth, the race shall take place on the day stated above at the door of the cañada of this city, from the place where there are some rocks, departing from said rocks, to 10 varas upon the city limits, start shall be from one to two o'clock p.m. with the word to start

PORTRAIT OF DON JOSÉ ANDRÉS SEPÚLVEDA
*(Painted by the French artist Penelone about 1856;
Charles W. Bowers Memorial Museum, Santa Ana)*

SHEEP ON THE IRVINE RANCH (BEFORE 1958)

"Santiago" the race horses free at one only shriek, and to secure the fulfillment of this contract, both parties obligate themselves that the party that does not run shall forfeit 150 head of cattle, and this obligation shall be firm and valid, and for this object the party which takes default shall be bound equally as under any other obligation which is established by the laws.

In testimony of which we subscribe our names and place our seals, in the city and date above stated.

There is one condition of this contract, that if Don Andrés Pico loses he shall deliver the cattle on the ranch of Santa Margarita the 15th day of November, and if Don Fernando Sepúlveda loses he shall deliver the cattle on the ranch of San Joaquín by the same day, the 15th of November.

The starting word "Santiago" has to be given from behind the horses that run.

Thus we agree date as above. The horses are also staked in the race.

Gambling losses, extravagances of dress, too lavish hospitality—whatever the cause, the owner of the Rancho San Joaquin was soon caught in a slough of debt from which he never successfully escaped. A rough memorandum of the early fifties lists the names of at least a dozen creditors to whom José Sepúlveda owed a total of over $7,000, in amounts running from a few hundred dollars to over four thousand. Interest rates on these notes were four, five, six, and seven per cent a month—compounded!—and the list contained only a few of the ranchero's many debts.

In 1855, the prodigal-spending Don José placed a mortgage for $15,000 on the Rancho San Joaquin with Samuel Mors, Jr. The interest rate was three and a half per cent a month. Shortly after paying back this loan, Sepúlveda and his wife, Francisca, borrowed $10,000 from the ex-trapper, Santa Fe trader, and distinguished pueblo citizen William Wolfskill. The note, secured by mortgage on the Rancho

San Joaquin, ran for one year and called for monthly interest payments of two per cent. The document is signed, "José Sepulveda" and "Francisca Abila de Sepulveda, her X mark," the X being, of course, the sign of the Cross.

The Sepúlveda note to Wolfskill was paid before it fell due, but in October 1860, Don José and Doña Francisca borrowed $6,000 again on mortgage, from Baruch Marks, a prosperous Los Angeles merchant who had a store in Mellus' or Bell's Row, a long adobe building on the east side of Los Angeles Street between First and Aliso. The note ran for six months, and the interest was two per cent a month.

In the mortgage, the Rancho San Joaquin was said to contain "eleven square leagues of land, more or less," and to have the following boundaries: "Beginning at a hill on the edge of the Sea beach and running Northerly through the Cañada de la Laguna 15,400 varas to the 'Arroyo del Toro' thence Westerly 17,900 varas to the 'Cerrito de las Ranas' thence from a stone pillar Southerly with the line of the 'Rancho de Santa Ana' 19,150 varas to a point on the Sea Beach, so as to include the 'Bolsa de San Joaquin' thence Easterly along the Sea Beach 14,500 varas to the point of beginning."

Two months, or a little more, after obtaining the loan from Marks, Sepúlveda gave Wolf Kalisher of Los Angeles a second mortgage on the ranch in return for a six months' loan of $5,000 bearing interest at two and a half per cent a month. On May 23, 1864, both Marks and Kalisher brought suit to foreclose their respective mortgages and satisfy the notes. Judgment was rendered against the Sepúlvedas in the amount of $7,581 to Marks and $11,464 to Kalisher.

Presumably borrowing funds from some other source, the debt-ridden ranchero succeeded in paying the two judgments, but his time was running out. On December 6, 1864,

when the Great Drought was at its height, Don José Sepúlveda, symbol of an era—brief, colorful as a desert sky at sunset, and touched with the pathos of a past that never can
return—sold the Rancho San Joaquin, a principality of elev-
en square leagues or fifty thousand acres, more or less, for
eighteen thousand dollars "and other valuable considera-
tions."[1]

The purchasers, who held the ranch as tenants-in-common, were James Irvine of San Francisco and the three prosperous sheepmen of northern California who had recently
transferred their activities to Los Angeles County—Llewellyn Bixby and Benjamin and Thomas Flint. Bixby and the
Flints operated under a partnership known as Flint, Bixby
and Company. Thomas Flint and Llewellyn Bixby each
owned three twentieths of the ranch, Benjamin Flint four
twentieths, and James Irvine the remaining fifty per cent.
The four partners continued to own and operate the ranch
until 1876 when Irvine bought out the other three.

The Rancho Lomas de Santiago, third of the land grants
that were consolidated to form the Irvine Ranch, was the
last of the three to be approved by the Land Commission.
Its title, at the time, was free of all legal entanglements. It
was bounded, according to the Commission-approved petition, by the Santiago hills on the east, "the Serrito de Las
Ranas and the boundary of the San Joaquin on the west, the
Rancho del Toro on the south, and on the north by the
Rancho of Santa Ana, as delineated on the map."

The land included within these boundaries was defined
as "4 square leagues, more or less." But as later surveys
showed, the designated boundaries included far more than

[1]The deed was recorded on December 7, 1864.

the area which the original petition specified, and this wide discrepancy became the basis of much subsequent confusion and litigation.

When the government, following the usual practice, appealed the Land Commission's confirmation of the grant of the Lomas de Santiago, the United States District Court, recognizing that "boundaries in a description are paramount," formally declared: "It is ordered and decreed that the decision of the Board of Land Commissioners is hereby affirmed and the claim of the District Court Appellee is good and valid, and the same be and hereby is confirmed to him to the extent of *eleven leagues* and no more, within the boundaries specified in the grant."[2]

Since no appeal was taken from the court's decision, a patent was eventually issued for the eleven square leagues, or 47,226.61 acres. Much of the huge tract was too rough and mountainous for cultivation, but the official survey carried the northern boundary of the ranch to the Santa Ana River, and the water rights thus acquired later became an extremely important asset.[3]

In 1860, four years after the federal court's confirmation of title, Teodosio Yorba and his wife, Inocencia Reyes de Yorba, accepted $7,000 for the ranch and put their marks on a deed that transferred the Lomas de Santiago, "bounded on the North by the Santa Ana River, East by the mountains, South by the Rancho Aliso, and West by the Rancho of San Joaquin" to William Wolfskill.

[2]The italics are the author's.

[3]The patent to the ranch was issued February 1, 1868. For a detailed discussion of the controversial area and boundaries of the Lomas de Santiago, see below, pp. 128-132, and the government publication, *Mexican Land Grant Frauds*, there cited and described.

— 44 —

Pioneer in the Santa Fe–Los Angeles trade and one of the two earliest founders of California's wine and fruit industries, Wolfskill was a gentleman of modesty, integrity, and enterprise to whom Los Angeles and southern California owed much of their development.

The owner of several other ranch properties in southern California, including the Rancho Santa Anita which had originally belonged to the "Scotch Paisano," Hugo Reid, and Victoria, his Indian wife, Wolfskill converted the Lomas de Santiago into a sheep ranch and held the grant until 1866. Just before his death the old fur trader then sold the property to the Flint-Bixby interests for $7,000—the same price that he himself had paid for it six years before.

Irvine may or may not have participated as a silent partner in the purchase of the Lomas de Santiago from Wolfskill. Two years later, in any event, he is listed as the owner of an undivided half interest in the eleven-square-league grant.

Except for a few minor transactions, the acquisition of the Lomas de Santiago rounded out the holdings of the Irvine-Flint-Bixby interests in southern California. In addition to the eleven-square-league Lomas de Santiago, they owned the equally large Rancho San Joaquin, the 3,800-acre strip of the Rancho Santiago de Santa Ana, and other smaller properties. The total area of their holdings came to about 110,000 acres.

6

A LAWLESS LAND

When Irvine, Bixby, and the Flints acquired their landholdings in the Santa Ana Valley, the region was losing its
rude, culturally impoverished character and gradually taking on the traits of a stable, well-organized society. Less
than a decade earlier, however, all of southern California
had been a lawless, bandit-ridden frontier, and even as late
as 1871, a Los Angeles mob, "composed of the scum and
dregs of the city," massacred between twenty and twenty-
five Chinese; and Tiburcio Vasquez, last of the notorious
Spanish-California bandit leaders, was not captured until
1874. Murder and robbery, in the fifties and early sixties,
were commonplace; wholesale thefts of cattle and horses
cut heavily into the herds of the large rancheros; travel in
all parts of the country was rendered hazardous by outlaws
who lassoed and dragged unwary riders to death with their
reatas and by organized bands of highwaymen who preyed
especially upon stage coaches and small caravans.

The lawless, unsettled state of the country, in general,
was vividly illustrated by an experience of Don Juan Forster, later the owner of the Santa Margarita ranch. A letter
addressed to Abel Stearns in February 1852 speaks for itself.

Forster wrote in haste from the home of Don Teodosio
Yorba, probably on the Rancho Lomas de Santiago.

Dear Sir. Having arrived here about six o'clock and taken up my
quarters at Don Teodocio's house shortly after the house was taken
possession of by a party of deserted volunteers from San Diego
demanding to be provided with liquor using the most abusive and
threatening language and brandishing their arms, when being on the
point of shooting the man in charge of the establishment I offered
some words of pasification which they returned (determined to
take the life of somebody) with the same above abusive and ther-
eating terms and actually whent so far as to *toss up* amongst themselves for the chance as it might ocurr, as to which of the party
should shoot me and during the opperation I have been so fortunate
as to escape from the house.

Don Ramon Osuno with his family being in the house has had to
take to the *campo* [field] until this hour without any of us [having]
any covering. We are now in Doña Vicentas house momently expecting to be attacked.

This state of things is realy intolerable and I have taken the liberty to state the circumstance to you hoping you will circulate it
amongst our friends &c so as to see if there can be measurs concerted, to prevent in future such a dreadfull State of affairs.

Don Leandro Serranos family have also deserted their house and
have actually taken to the Guatamotal for protection.

(Excuse haste)

Some four or five years later, the wild hinterland of the
Lomas de Santiago and the Rancho San Joaquin—the high-
walled Santiago Cañon and the steep, rough peaks of the
Santa Ana range—witnessed one of the most extensive and
exciting man hunts in California annals.

At that time a formidable band of California or Mexican-
born outlaws, some of whom were former penitentiary in-
mates, led by Juan Flores and Pancho Daniel, took over the
little town of San Juan Capistrano, killed an inoffensive

storekeeper named George Pflugardt, looted a number of stores, and a day or two later rode off in the mountains toward Los Angeles.

Meanwhile, at least according to the most reliable version of the story, Forster sent a boy on horseback to Los Angeles with the report of Pflugardt's murder, and Sheriff John Barton, with a party of six men, set out for San Juan Capistrano. The company stopped at the house of Don José Sepúlveda on the Rancho San Joaquin. It is said that while the sheriff and his men were eating breakfast, Chola Martina, Flores' sweetheart, tampered with their guns, but this may have been a later addition to the story.

At any rate, either Sepúlveda or his *mayordomo* advised Barton that Flores and Daniel had at least fifty men in the mountains and that it would be folly for the small posse to go farther. Barton, however, attached little importance to the warning and continued on his way to San Juan. The Los Angeles *Star* of January 31, 1857, contained the following account of the ensuing tragedy:

When about twelve miles from Sepulveda's ranch, at a spur of the San Joaquin Ranch Mountains, they observed a man galloping along the plain, for a distance of a mile, off on the left of the road, when Little spoke to Baker, saying it would be better to ride forward and see what the man meant to do. When they had advanced about 400 yards ahead of the party, they were suddenly attacked by a band of robbers, at least twenty in number, who rushed out from between the hills. There is an arroyo on the left, between them and where the man had been seen galloping, but no one came to the attack from that quarter. When the guide saw robbers advancing, he called out, "these are the robbers, shoot them, shoot them."

Barton and the other three immediately rushed to the assistance of Little and Baker, but before they could reach them, the latter were killed. The four charged on the robbers, fired their guns, and

Barton his pistols, and then fought with it clubbed. One of the robbers was heard to say to Barton "G–d d—n you, I have got you now." To which Barton replied, "I reckon I have got you, too." Their guns were being leveled at each other during the remark, the discharge was simultaneous, but Barton fell, shot through the heart. Our informant states, that three of the robbers fell on the first discharge.

Daly, who was mounted on a mule, was cut off from his party in the charge to assist Baker and Little, was run for about three miles, and then overtaken and murdered.

Hardy, seeing Barton fall, called to Alexander, stating, also, that he had lost his pistol. There being only two left, and Hardy practically without arms, they broke and ran for their lives, and effected their escape, owing to the fleetness of their horses.

The robbers pursued them for twelve miles, till they came within sight of Sepulveda's house. For the first 400 yards of the chase, the balls whistled thick and fast around the fugitives, making the dust on the road fly up before and around them. The two stopped at the ranch to get a drink of water, and while there several shots were fired at the rear, supposed to be when the robbers had given up the chase and turned back.

At the time of the attack, there was another party on the left hand hill, but they did not come down. Mr. Alexander stopped at the Monte to inform the citizens, and Mr. Hardy came on to town with the intelligence.

The Effect of the Intelligence

On the arrival of Hardy, the news instantly spread over the town, and the most intense excitement prevailed throughout the community. It was at once resolved to arm and equip a party to go out in pursuit of the robbers and exterminate them, and within two hours, about forty men, well armed and mounted, started off in the good cause.

Recovery of the Bodies

On Saturday morning, another party, about fourteen in number on horseback and in carriages, started out to recover the dead bodies of the murdered men, taking with them four coffins in wagons.

The bodies of Barton and Baker were found within about ten feet of the lower road to San Juan—about a mile below the Rodeo de la Laguna, on the ranch of San Joaquin, on the near side of the small hills to the right of Arroyo de los Palos Verdes—on the Canyon del Alisal—about fifteen miles this side of the Mission of San Juan Capistrano. Barton's body was lying on the left side of the road with the head towards the road, and about 300 yards this side of Baker, who was lying on the right hand side of the road. Little's body was lying about 100 yards from Baker, at about right angles with the road. The body of C. F. Daly, the blacksmith, was found about three miles from the road, as if he had started to go to the middle Santa Ana road. Little's horse was found within ten steps of the body of Barton, shot through the heart on the off side. The pockets of all were rifled of their contents, the robbers becoming possessed of three gold watches and chains, valuable diamond pins and other jewelry. Barton's papers all torn in small pieces, which were collected and brought in.

Little's horse had the saddle on—Barton's boots were taken, his hat was near his body—the hats of Little and Baker were missing.

Barton's body had three wounds in the region of the heart, the left arm broken, and a shot in the right eye.

Little was shot in the right eye, head and body.

Baker was shot in back of head when aiming at Flores, also in right eye and cheek.

Daly shot in the mouth and body. The face burned with the powder. The bodies had evidently been fired upon, after death.

The murder of Barton and his companions caused intense indignation and excitement throughout all of southern California. Detachments of mounted rangers, companies of native Californians, federal troops, and Indian scouts joined a concerted movement to track down the outlaws and bring the whole band to justice.

A letter from Don Juan Forster to Dr. John S. Griffin of Los Angeles gives an interesting contemporary account of the early part of the proceedings:

San Juan 30th Jany 1857

Dr. Griffin

Dear Sir.

As Don Andres left here yesterday evening acting in concert with the force from the Monte, I take the liberty of answering his letter. . . .

Dn. Andres had such information (amounting to a certainty) that the Robbers where hidden in the Mountain of Santiago somewhere about the head of the Stream, and after obtaining a fresh supply of horses from Santa Margarita, and joining in concert with the Monte force they left here about dusk last evening, and by this time or this evening I have no doubt that they will have caught either all, or most of them, they have with them men, from this place well acquainted with every nook & corner of the Mountain & I can see no possible chance of their escaping excepting they should take the direction of Los Angeles, as we have a very strong force posted in every pass and Mountain between this place & San Luis [Rey], for instance, there is 40 Dragoons, some citizens from San Diego, the indian Manuelito with upwards of 50 indians posted on the Mountain, and between that and the Flores, Geronimo is also upon the alert in the country about Temeculo, so that there is no possible chance of their escaping down South.

It is reported that the wounded robbers have been sent to Los Angeles so they must be looked out for. . . .

According to information the Robbers are not by any means as strong as they have been represented.

The bearer has orders that in case of meeting any force from Los Angeles to request their leader to open this so as to obtain what information I can impart, for his government.

The Los Angeles *Star*, in its issues of January 31 and February 7, gave a detailed account of the organization of the different companies, the pursuit of the bandits, and the various engagements with scattered bands in the Santa Ana Mountains.

Flores himself was captured, early in the pursuit, with Sheriff Barton's gold watch still in his possession. According to the *Star*, the capture was effected by a posse from El Monte and a company of thirty-five Californians, some of whom were armed with lances, led by Don Andrés Pico. A band of forty-three Indians under their captain, Manuelito, also served as scouts.

The detailed newspaper account read as follows:

The first step taken was to send Indian spies into the mountains, to find the camp of the robbers. One of the runners returned before dark the same day, and reported that the camp was situated at the head of the Canada de Santiago. A second spy came in during the night, and reported to Don Andres that he had conversed with one of the band, Antonio Ma. Varelas (Chino) who sent word to Don Andres, to place his men in a certain position, and he would be sure to catch the whole gang. The moon, however, going down at an early hour, prevented the execution of the plan. Early next morning, the party marched to the place designated, but as they were taking up their position, Flores crept to an overhanging rock, observed the movement, and commenced a retreat into the mountain fastnesses. Don Andres then charged up the mountain after him, Flores driving Chino before him, with his gun leveled on him. The Chino was prevented by Flores from joining the Californians, till the arrival of Dr. Gentry's party of Americans, when being engaged in arraying his men, Chino effected his escape to Don Tomas Sanchez. Shots were exchanged by the parties, but at too great a distance to take effect.

Flores and his men climbed up a very high peak of the mountain on horseback and two went up afoot. Don Andres disposed his men along the side of the mountain, so as to guard the robbers, and dispatched a runner for the Americans who were encamped in the Trabujo Pass. On their arrival, they divided into two parties—that under Dr. Gentry guarding the mountain, while the other, under Mr. B. Copewood, made the attack.

The mountain to which the robbers had fled, was almost inaccessible, even on foot, and while the Americans were ascending the hill, Juan Flores, Jesus Espinosa, and Leonardo Lopez slid their horses down a precipice to a kind of shelf about fifty feet below, where they abandoned them and escaped down a precipitous ledge of rocks, about 500 feet high, by aid of the brush growing on its side. Thence, they took refuge in the adjacent mountain, making their way through dense chaparral on foot.

Francisco Ardillero, attempting to escape down the mountain, was captured by Gentry's party.

Juan Silvas, fearing to make the desperate leap with Flores and his two companions, and knowing that he could not evade the guards, gave himself up to the Californians.

When the company left the scene of the attack it was sundown; they went to the foot of the mountain and encamped, and learned that night from Chino that Francisco Daniel, Andres Fontes, Santos (since shot at the Mission) and the Piquinini, had gone to Los Angeles.

Next morning a party under Don Tomas Sanchez, started for the city, with the Chino as a guide to point out their hiding place. The remainder of the party kept up a strict guard on the various mountain passes.

Don Andres returned to San Juan, obtained the assistance of the Indians and scoured the mountains.

Dr. Gentry's party discovered the trail of Flores and his associates, pursued it and came in sight of them, when the robbers attempted to evade them by hiding in a cave in the canada. From this, they fired on their pursuers, wounding one of the party, Francis Goddard. Seeing that they were at last caught, and overpowered by numbers, they made no further attempt to escape, and surrendered.

The prisoners were taken to the San Joaquin Ranch, about five or six miles from where they were captured, tied up, presumably with rawhide thongs, and placed under guard for the night.

About midnight, however, thanks to the carelessness of the guard, Flores and some others escaped and again took to the mountains.

Meanwhile, Don Andrés Pico, who was especially active

in the pursuit and breakup of the band, was scouring the mountains for the remnant of the fugitives. When he was informed of the escape of Flores and his companions, the *Star* naïvely adds, "Don Andres, not wishing to risk the safety of his prisoners hung Silvas and Ardillero. He then divided his forces and diligently searched the whole country from San Juan to the Los Angeles River."

Flores, with no weapons and only a little dried beef for food, poorly mounted, and wounded in the right arm, was recaptured in a rugged pass between the San Fernando and Simi valleys, nearly a hundred miles from the scene of Sheriff Barton's murder. The young outlaw was taken to Los Angeles, and there a popular tribunal, consisting of most of the citizens of the pueblo and many representatives from other communities and ranchos, voted for his immediate execution. The *Star* of February 21, 1857, contained the following account of the gruesome episode:

When the meeting adjourned, the people marched to the jail, and took possession of Flores. He had been expecting this visit. In a short time he was led out, and was received by Capt. Twist's company who guarded him to the place of execution. These were followed by Capt. Farget's company (French) the whole escorted by a large company of mounted Californians and Americans. The Rev. Father Raho and Rev. Vicente Llover, were also in attendance, and accompanied the prisoner to his last scene. The prisoner walked with firmness and seemed as composed as any one in the crowd. The distance from the jail to the hill on which the scaffold was erected, is about a quarter of a mile. The prisoner was dressed in white pants, light vest, and black merino sack coat. He was a young man, about twenty-two years of age, and of pleasing countenance. There was nothing in his appearance to indicate the formidable bandit which he had proved himself to be.

On arriving at the place of execution, the prisoner was led to the foot of the gallows, still accompanied by his spiritual guides, the armed men forming a hollow square, supported by the cavalry in rear. His arms were then tied to his body and thus pinioned, he firmly ascended the drop. He expressed a wish to address the people, who instantly became silent. His remarks were interpreted, and were merely to the effect—that he was now ready to die—that he had committed many crimes—that he died without having ill-will against any man, and hoped that no one would bear ill-will against him. He repeated that he was now ready to die. Observing some persons among the crowd whom he had known, he called one or two towards him, and gave some final directions leaving his body to them. He then handed a white handkerchief to one of the attendants, and wished his face to be covered with it, which was done. His legs were then bound, and the rope adjusted around his neck, during which he continued in conversation with those in his immediate vicinity. The handkerchief was placed over his head, the attendants took farewell of him, left the drop, and immediately after the plank was drawn from under him, and the body of Flores swung in the air. The fall was too short, and the unfortunate wretch struggled in agony for a considerable time. In his last, despairing efforts, the rope around his arms slipped above his elbows, and he grasped the rope by which he was suspended. It required considerable effort to release his hold. After a protracted struggle, very painful to behold, the limbs became quiet and finally stiff in death. Thus ended the brief but stormy life of the bandit captain, Juan Flores. After hanging some time, a physician examined the body and declared that there was no pulse. The body was kept hanging for about an hour and was then handed over to those who had engaged to take charge of it.

After which, the people dispersed. The execution took place about two o'clock P.M.

Pancho Daniel, co-commander of the outlaw band, was captured sometime later and hanged, without the sentence of a formal court, late in November or early in December 1858. All in all, some twelve or fifteen members of this famous outlaw band who terrorized much of the settled portion of southern California from Santa Barbara to San Diego and made its last stand in Santiago Cañon and the Santa Ana Mountains over a hundred years ago thus paid the price of lawlessness and often ruthless crime.

The breakup of the Flores-Daniel band by no means marked the end of lawlessness and violence on what is now the Irvine Ranch. The holes and cavities in the soft rock of Frémont Cañon, a branch of the Santiago, are still known as "Robbers Caves." At the mouth of the same cañon, a posse once captured and executed a band of horse thieves, cut off their ears to use as evidence, and left the lifeless bodies hanging from the trees!

Sheriff's Spring, a water hole on the landward side of the hills behind Corona del Mar, is said to take its name from a grim example of justice in the late sixties. After holding up the San Diego stage and carrying off the strongbox, five bandits rode to the spring and made camp for the night. Early in the morning, the sheriff and a posse quietly surrounded the unsuspecting band and killed all five before they had opportunity either to return the fire or escape. The strongbox, however, was mysteriously missing when the sheriff and his men examined the outlaw camp and—since every old California rancho must have its romantic tale of lost or buried treasure—if local tradition may be relied upon, the bandits' loot still lies hidden in the vicinity of Sheriff's Spring!

CATTLE ON THE IRVINE RANCH
(Photograph by Hollywood Studios, Santa Ana)

THE IRVINE COVE AT LAGUNA BEACH (BEFORE 1950)

7

IRVINE, BIXBY, AND THE FLINTS

The four northern Californians who bought the ranchos San Joaquin and Lomas de Santiago and the eight-mile-long strip of the Santiago de Santa Ana, after the devastating drought of the mid-sixties had made a desert of the ranges, were sheepmen instead of cattlemen, and their chief purpose in acquiring the Santa Ana basin ranchos was to engage in the production of wool on a large scale.

The two Flints and their cousin, Llewellyn Bixby, were of typical Maine colonial stock. Like thousands of other young men, they joined the Gold Rush of 1849, made a little money, returned home, and presently came back to live in California. The Maine adventurers' second trip to California, however, was very different from their first. In 1849 they had gone to California by sea to look for gold. In May 1853 they left Keokuk, Iowa, with a flock of nearly two thousand head of sheep, eleven yoke of oxen, two cows, four horses, two wagons, and complete camping equipment, to cross the continent.

The venture, if not foolhardy, was at least uncommonly daring, but by the exercise of constant vigilance and the aid of a large measure of good fortune, in eight months the three drovers brought their far-ranging flock to California without serious mishap and laid the foundation of a great industry and a great fortune.

Under the name of Flint, Bixby and Company, the three joined with Colonel W. W. Hollister to buy the 54,000-acre Rancho San Justo in Monterey County and thereafter rapidly expanded their holdings both of land and sheep.

The sheep industry yielded large returns before 1860, and with the disruption of the cotton trade during the Civil War, the resulting increase in the price of wool brought the California sheepmen still greater profit. According to Hittell, the total annual cost of herding, pasturing, shearing, and providing for the general care of a flock of sheep during this period was about thirty-five cents a head. Each animal yielded an average of six and a half pounds of wool, which normally brought the grower from eighteen to thirty-five cents a pound. Such profits produced substantial fortunes in a few years.

Soon after the opening of the Civil War, a number of the largest of the wool growers in Monterey, Santa Cruz, and adjacent counties sought to extend their operations farther south and either lease or purchase some of the large cattle ranchos near Los Angeles. The drought of the mid-sixties played directly into the hands of these outsiders, and by the close of the Civil War the sheep industry was firmly established in a number of the southern counties. James Irvine and Flint, Bixby and Company were among the largest of the landowners who chose to put sheep instead of cattle on their newly acquired ranges.[1]

[1]Irvine bought little or no land in southern California outside of what is now Orange County, but the Flint-Bixby company and other members of the Bixby family acquired extensive holdings in various other sections. These included Juan

James Irvine, the dominant figure in the partnership of Irvine, Bixby, and the Flints, was of Scotch-Irish Presbyterian ancestry—the strong, tenacious, God-fearing stock that contributed so much to the founding of the United States and the creation of American institutions. Irvine was born in Belfast, Ireland, December 27, 1827. His father was a man of modest income; and as James was next to the youngest in a family of nine children, he could later write with deep feeling and understanding, "I tell you a boy cast upon the world with not a dollar in his pocket, with none within reach . . . but absolute strangers and without . . . a claim upon any of them is in a position to appreciate the value of a helping hand."

Irvine came to the United States with his younger brother, William, in 1846 and worked for two years in the Praslee Paper Mills at Molden Bridge, New York. In 1849 he joined the gold stampede to California and elected to go by way of the Isthmus of Panama. The *Humboldt*, on which he obtained passage after crossing the Isthmus, was a wretched excuse for a vessel and required a hundred and one days to reach San Francisco. Among his companions on the voyage were Collis P. Huntington, who later became the dominant member of the group known as the "Big Four," builders of the Central and Southern Pacific railroads, and Dr. Benjamin Flint. Irvine's chance association with the latter passenger apparently started the long sequence of events that eventually led to the creation of the Irvine Ranch.

Temple's Rancho Los Cerritos of 27,000 acres; the neighboring and slightly larger Rancho Los Alamitos, recently the possession of Abel Stearns; half of the Sepúlveda 32,000-acre Rancho Palos Verdes; and eventually the 36,000-acre Rancho San Juan Cajon de Santa Ana, which had been granted to Don Pacífico Ontiveras in 1837.

Once in California, Irvine struck out for the gold fields where for a time he filled the dual role of merchant and miner. In the meantime, one of his kinsmen named John Lyons opened a commission house in San Francisco on Front Street, and in 1854 Irvine bought an interest in the business. Thereafter, until 1857, the firm was listed in the San Francisco directory as "Irvine & Co., wholesale produce and grocery mchts." The profits of the business were large, and Irvine invested heavily in income-producing real estate in San Francisco.

Lyons withdrew from the firm in 1866, and three years later Irvine sold part of his interests to his brother, William, and an associate named Asa Harker. The name of the firm was then changed to Irvine, Harker & Co. In 1873 James Irvine withdrew entirely from active participation in the partnership and thereafter devoted his time to his San Francisco properties, his southern California holdings, and his other large investments.

On July 25, 1866, Irvine married Nettie Rice of Cleveland, Ohio,[2] and the couple made their home at the corner of Folsom and Eleventh streets, in San Francisco. The house, with its furnishings, cost upwards of $25,000, "but it is a very comfortable one," Irvine wrote, "with a beautiful yard filled with shrubbery, flowers, and clover and there I take solid enjoyment."[3]

Mrs. Irvine came of a distinguished family. Her father, Harvey Rice, was born at the beginning of the century in Conway, Massachusetts, and at the age of twenty-four,

[2]Some years earlier Irvine's father and mother had come from Belfast to live in Cleveland, and he was well acquainted in that city.

[3]In 1875 Irvine built fourteen or fifteen houses near the site of his new home for rental purposes.

after graduating from Williams College, joined the rapidly increasing migration to Ohio. The young New Englander reached Cleveland, then a frontier settlement of four hundred inhabitants, with "a letter of introduction to a leading citizen of the town, a college diploma printed in Latin . . . , a scanty supply of wearing apparel, a few classical textbooks, and a three dollar bank-note."

After serving his apprentice years in Ohio as a schoolteacher, Rice became in turn a successful lawyer, real-estate salesman, public official, and prolific author. As state senator he took an active part in badly needed prison reform, and—a matter of much greater significance—became gratefully known to his fellow citizens as the "Father of the Common School System of Ohio." At a time when education was a luxury reserved for the well-to-do, Rice sought to make the common schools "the colleges of the people—'cheap enough for the poorest, and good enough for the richest,'" and thus to create "a democracy of knowledge" in which there should be true brotherhood and equality among men. One would like to know how greatly Ohio today is indebted for the state's extraordinary number of colleges and universities to the philosophy and leadership of Nettie Rice Irvine's versatile and democratic father.

In his business affairs, James Irvine was known for sagacity, sound judgment, sense of fairness and justice, and his "exactitude even in the most trivial transactions." He was deeply concerned for the welfare of his parents and the large family of brothers and sisters still living in Ireland. He advised them on many problems, sent them money from time to time, and, finally, on December 16, 1869, wrote to his brother John that he had "been blessed with a great degree of prosperity" and knew of no better way in which to use his wealth than to aid others less fortunate and share it with other members of his family, even though some of them might not actually require such assistance. He added that he had accordingly decided to set aside from £500 to £1,000 annually for his kinsfolk, distributing it where he thought it was most needed, would do the most good, or would confer the most happiness.

Irvine also financed a number of his brothers in different business ventures; at very considerable personal inconvenience assisted J. H. Hollister, one of the pioneer sheepmen of California, when the latter was hard pressed for funds; and generously came to the aid of an older man who had once befriended him but later incurred financial losses that cost Irvine himself a matter of $10,000. Irvine's letter in reference to this matter is self-explanatory:

San Francisco, December 20, 1870

My Dear Mr. Hanna:

The accompanying letter is written with reference to business solely and quite as much in Flint Bixby & Co.'s interests as my own. This postscript is without any reference and purely a matter between you and myself.

As I understand it now (of course from hearsay) your fortune will be entirely absorbed in the wreck of your business so nothing will be left you. At your time of life this is too hard, and recuperation hardly to be thought of, indeed hardly to be attempted.

Under the circumstances I feel at liberty to make the following proposition, only asking you to receive it in the spirit it is written in and intended.

You extended aid and kindness to me when they were needed and valuable. For my position in life today I feel much under obligation to you. I have never yet ceased to entertain a deep sense of gratitude for your kindly aid and kindness. . . .

But now is my turn to make more substantial acknowledgement of gratitude and I do it with a great deal of pleasure. You are advanced in years and reverses have made you poor, I am but in middle life, fortune has been kind to me and I am comparatively rich therefore able to aid you and I mean to do it. I mean that you shall never want for a necessary comfort of life so long as I have means to supply it. To that end I tender you a home in my family as long as you live which I trust you will accept. If I cannot persuade you to accept this then tell me how much you require to support you in such position in life as you may choose, and I will endeavor to see that your wants are supplied.

Now I hope you will in no event be offended with the proposition.

Irvine's appreciation of the value of education was typical of his Presbyterian Scotch-Irish upbringing and early environment. Referring to the children of one of his brothers who were attending a good school despite death and illness in the family, he thoughtfully wrote: "Undoubtedly in their more mature years they will have more to thank their parents for and will feel more deeply and thoroughly grateful for the opportunity and means afforded them for obtaining a good education, than for anything else that may or can be given them. That lasts and blesses for life, and to a certain extent commands success. It certainly aids it greatly, while a little or even a large sum of money may last but a short time and prove of little value while it does."

Of the thousands of strangers who poured into California during the stirring years that followed Marshall's discovery of gold, none became more enamored of the new land than James Irvine. "Flowers," he wrote, "bloom here throughout the year in the open air and fresh vegetables in an almost endless variety are to be had in our markets in winter as in summer." Green peas, new potatoes, lettuce, strawberries, and oranges were available in mid-January, and the California climate was far superior to that of Italy.

"Can you wonder," he wrote an English baronet, "that I like to live in such a country—a country that . . . is one of the most prosperous on the globe?"

Even a major earthquake, one of the severest the state has experienced, could not check such artless enthusiasm. The temblor occurred on October 21, 1868, did serious damage in San Francisco, and killed a large number of people. In a letter to one of his brothers, Irvine gave a graphic description of the disaster:

The ground sunk from a few inches to several feet, and in other places it opened and closed again, testing buildings severely. There was of course a general rush for the streets and elsewhere to get out of the way of the falling walls. Thousands of chimneys were either tumbled down, broken off at the roof, or twisted around. Some friends were at my house and we were at breakfast at the time. All felt the shake and were about to make a hasty retreat, I urged them to sit still, that it would be over in a few seconds. They did so for a short time but the shock continued, becoming steadily more severe until the house sounded as if it were being wrenched and ground to pieces. With one consent all sprang to their feet and ran to get out of doors in which they soon succeeded. I ran upstairs for Baby and the nurse and when we got down it was all over. We all escaped injury, narrowly missing a lot of falling plaster that fell in the hall where we were running. After the shock I went on an exploring expedition to see how the house had stood it and in nearly every room found abundant evidence of rough usage in the shape of fallen plaster, cracked walls, vases and other articles thrown down and in some cases broken. On ascending to the roof I found the chimneys (of which there were four tall heavy ones) broken near the roof and some of them moved quite out of place. Fortunately none of them fell down as in that case there is not much doubt but that they would have gone through the house, clear to the cellar before stopping, and ruined the house. They weighed three to four tons each above the roof. I have had them taken down and others newer and lighter and not so tall put in their places and now we feel much safer. Our house like nearly all the residences here is built of wood so there [is] not much damage to any part of it except the brick chimneys being thrown down. I would not live in a brick or stone house. I have felt many earthquakes before but this one beats them all. I hope we shall have no more like it. The business portion of the city, built of bricks, stone and iron suffered severely, but much less than I would have supposed. . . .

The earth don't seem quite settled yet, some 30 to 40 shakes have occurred since the heavy one (3 of them within the last 24 hours) but none heavy enough to do any harm except to keep some people nervous.

Severe though the earthquake was, San Francisco took it in stride. A severe epidemic of smallpox a few months later and an incidental outbreak of scarlet fever failed to check the city's amazing growth or force a business depression. In the state as a whole, mining had long since yielded the pre-eminent place to agriculture, the first transcontinental railroad was nearing completion, building and manufacturing in San Francisco were never before so active. On Montgomery, California, Bush, and a few other streets real estate was selling at from $500 to $3,000 a front foot. In two years' time Irvine's own city property had risen in value to nearly $200,000. It is small wonder that the once poor boy of Belfast thought California the "most prosperous and progressive state in the Union."[4]

The birth of a son and heir on October 16, 1867, added greatly to Irvine's happiness.[5] The boy was named for his father; but Irvine's rejoicing was soon cut short by his wife's

[4]Irvine was a member of the Vigilance Committee of 1856, a stanch Republican, and a prominent figure in the Society of California Pioneers, an organization that has profited from the financial counsel and support of three generations of the Irvine family.

[5]A second son, Harvey Rice, was born in March 1874 but lived only about seven months.

critical illness from puerperal fever, the dreaded curse of childbirth in that pre-antiseptic age. For some hours it was touch and go whether the young mother would live or die, and Irvine could not find words to express his relief and gratitude when the crisis passed.

To his wife's mother he wrote: "I am going to do all in my power to benefit or make her happy. I love her too dearly to do otherwise, and daily I feel grateful to you and her father for the wife you gave me, for I think a sweeter nature and lovelier spirit than hers God never breathed into human form."

Irvine's admiration for true goodness and his scorn for hypocrisy and sham appeared in the same letter. "We feel greatly indebted to Aunt Jennie Rice for the very kind part she has taken in our time of need," he wrote. "She professed little but performed much. Her religion springs as much from a good heart & noble mind as from her Bible, and without some such support shall I say that I think Bible Christianity will not give out the ring of the true metal though one could repeat texts and passages from it by the hour."

In contrast to this good woman, Irvine spoke of another who was always liberal in advice, "professions of sympathy, affectionate regard and tenderness, anxious and watchful care, etc, etc, etc," but whose helpfulness and religion began and ended there. "From her," he continued, with ill-concealed contempt, "we have learned long since to expect nothing but professions & . . . personally I may say I am not fond of professions."

One may say with reasonable confidence that the founder of the Irvine Ranch did not like a hypocrite.

8

CONSOLIDATION

Though his grocery and produce business in San Francisco proved highly profitable and his real-estate investments rose rapidly in value, Irvine's larger fortune lay in the lands he and his associates, Flint, Bixby and Company, had acquired in southern California. Irvine's ownership of as large an interest in the properties as the other three combined made him the dominant factor in the group and probably its financial mainstay as well.

In accordance with a plan previously agreed upon, the four partners immediately stocked their newly acquired ranchos with thousands of head of sheep. Irvine visited the ranches in the summer of 1867 and went back to San Francisco a confirmed enthusiast. "We rode about a good deal," he wrote, "sometimes coming home in the evening after a 30 or 40 miles ride pretty thoroughly tired out, but we had to do it in order to see much of the ranch and the flock. We have been making further purchases of land adjoining ours. Now our tract contains about 101- to 115,000 acres. On one side the line is nearly 23 miles long and the average width is nearly 8 miles. So you see there is considerable riding to be done, if one is to see much of it."

The winter rains were generous that year, and Irvine found enough feed on the ranges to support two hundred thousand head of sheep. The partners were then grazing fewer than thirty thousand but expected to have ten or fifteen thousand more within the next six or eight months and eventually raise the number to a hundred thousand and keep it permanently at about that level. The land itself also was rising rapidly in value and gave promise of continuing to appreciate for many years to come.

Probably as a result of this visit, Irvine urged the purchase of more and more sheep and stressed particularly the desirability of improving the standard of the flocks by the addition of thoroughbred bucks and ewes. A few months later the company imported some twenty-five Spanish Merinos at a cost of from two hundred and fifty to five hundred dollars each.

The winter of 1867-68 witnessed an abnormally high rainfall in southern California, so high indeed that both the San Gabriel and Santa Ana rivers changed their courses, many roads became impassable, and sheep on the Irvine-Flint-Bixby ranches suffered in some measure from the severity of the weather. The lamb crop, however, numbered between forty and forty-five thousand.

The partners shipped their wool from Newport Bay to San Francisco and there transshipped it to New York or Boston. Once the wool was in the eastern markets, Irvine insisted that it should be sold as promptly as possible since he had no desire "either to hold the goods or speculate on future markets." Prices remained high during 1868, and Irvine believed that after the ranches had been fully stocked they would yield a yearly "nett revenue of twenty to thirty thousand pounds sterling."

In November 1869, Harvey Rice, Irvine's father-in-law, spent the greater part of a week on the San Joaquin, as the holdings were then commonly called, and in a small but interesting book, *Letters from the Pacific Slope,* published the following year, thus described the great estate:

This ranch consists of one hundred and ten thousand acres, and is stocked with forty thousand fine-wooled sheep. In extent, it is one of the largest ranches south of Los Angeles, being some twelve miles wide by twenty long. It is mostly valley land, and stretches from the foot-hills to the sea. In some of the hills, within its boundaries, mines of coal and quicksilver have recently been discovered, which promise to become valuable. The ranch is amply watered by springs, and a chain of small lagoons, extending through it, centrally, supposed to be a subterranean river, from the connection there is in the hidden currents that pass from one lagoon to another, and the tremulous character of the soil, which seems to rest on its surface. In some places, if you thrust a pole through the turf, it disappears at once, and is never seen again.

These lagoons terminate in a small bay, which extends from the ocean into the ranch about two miles. On the shore of this bay I saw a camp of Mexican fishermen, who were engaged in manufacturing oil from the carcasses of sharks, which they catch in abundance along the sea coast. The Mexicans make this a profitable business. They go out to sea in small boats, and catch the sharks by harpooning or shooting them, as they rise to the surface in their eagerness to swallow the bait flung to them. When caught, they are towed into the bay, and so great is the number of their skeletons lying about the camp, that the atmosphere, throughout the entire vicinity for miles, is rendered impure and even offensive. . . .

The sheep with which this ranch is stocked, are subdivided in flocks of three thousand to five thousand, and each division placed in charge of a shepherd, who watches over them, by day and by night, like the shepherds of old, but with this difference, perhaps, that he gathers the sheep into a corral or pen at night, and then betakes himself to his eight-by-ten board cabin, next the enclosure, and there cooks, eats and sleeps as best he can, with no other associates than his sheep and faithful dog. His life is truly a lonely one, and yet he seems happy in the companionship of his sheep and dog, who understand his signs and his whistle, and even the import of his words, and obey him with a child-like confidence in his superior wisdom and intelligence. The annual clip of wool from the sheep of this ranch is said to be about two hundred thousand pounds. It is of the finest quality, and sells at a high price in the eastern market. Add to the income from the wool the annual product of twenty thousand lambs, and it is easy to see that wool-growing is a very profitable business in California.

As the months passed, James Irvine became more and more enthusiastic over the region in which the ranches were situated and spoke of it as the most delightful land he had ever seen "either in California or outside of it." His enthusiasm found expression, moreover, in concrete action as well as glowing phrases. To the partners' already princely landholdings, he quietly added numerous tracts in the "Santa Anas" and elsewhere in the neighborhood until he and his associates held an empire of nearly a hundred and twenty thousand acres, much of which was potential farming land of great fertility and value.

In the meantime, Los Angeles and the rich San Gabriel and Santa Ana valleys began to experience one of the first clearly defined real-estate booms in the history of southern California. A number of factors accounted for this sudden forward movement. The post–Civil War westward advance of settlement, stimulated in part by the anticipated completion of the Pacific Railroad, was well under way. Hundreds of Southern families, impoverished by the Civil War or unwilling to face the humiliation and harsh conditions imposed by Reconstruction, were looking to California as the land of new hope and opportunity. Publicity and advertising, of which California has received a larger share than perhaps any other corner of the globe, were making the state widely known in Europe as well as in the United States, and emigrant companies were being organized in Holland, Denmark, Germany, and the British Isles to settle in California. Even the commissioner of the United States General Land Office in Washington was moved to write to one such colonizing company and give the following inviting picture of the half-fabulous region near Los Angeles:

It will be observed that the good lands of Southern California are found on the Pacific . . . extending inland from twenty-five to seventy-five miles, embracing an area susceptible of cultivation and admirably adapted to horticulture, equal in extent to the State of Massachusetts.

The climate of these valleys, some little distance from the coast, is not surpassed in any portion of the world. . . . Numerous streams of water flow through these valleys—many of them permanent—furnishing the means of irrigating large bodies of land. The grape vine flourishes here luxuriantly. . . .

But the soil and climate of these valleys are equally well adapted to the growth of the orange, lemon, lime, citron, fig, walnut, olive, banana, almond, filbert, and currant; and wheat, barley, corn, potatoes, cotton, tobacco, and sugar cane thrive well. In an orange grove of 2,000 trees, near Los Angeles, the annual crop averages 1,500 oranges to each tree, some of the trees producing as many as 4,000 each. The sides and summits of the mountains contain an abundance of pine, cedar, hemlock, maple, and oak; and deposits of gold, silver, copper, tin, marble, alabaster, asphaltum, sulphur, salt and coal are numerous. . . .

Hundreds of thousands of acres of the finest lands, blest with a climate equal to that of the fairest portions of Italy, are held under Mexican grants, and are either entirely unoccupied or devoted to grazing; the proprietors, however, manifesting a willingness to subdivide and sell their claims as rapidly as the increase of settlers creates a demand.

As a result of these and other factors, Los Angeles County experienced a large increase of homeseekers, settlers, and small farmers. The resulting demand for land led to the subdivision of many of the old Spanish-Mexican grants near Los Angeles and brought about such an increase in values that ranches which had been assessed at ten cents an acre during the drought and considered highly priced at a dollar an acre as late as 1866 now readily sold at ten times the latter figure.

In January 1869, Irvine wrote that though much of the ranch land recently acquired by the partnership was "in active demand at ten dollars an acre and upwards," he and his associates had no intention of selling the ranches, at least for the time being, as prices were steadily rising. Taxes on the land temporarily lagged behind the increase in market values. In 1868 the Irvine-Flint holdings were assessed at about $28,000 and paid slightly less than $1,200 in county taxes. During that year the ranches produced some 70,000 pounds of wool that brought around thirty cents a pound in Boston and New York. But, in spite of these satisfactory returns, Irvine found the southern properties a source of many minor irritations.

Squatters began to move in on the ranches—as indeed they did on large holdings in many other parts of the state; the controversy between landowner and pre-emptor became increasingly bitter; and in many cases the quarrel led to violence and bloodshed.

Dissatisfaction with lighterage charges and delay in the settlement of an old account for damages led Irvine and his partners to transfer their shipping business from Newport Bay to Phineas Banning's new harbor of Wilmington. Wages and ranch costs were rising; taxes on at least part of

ENTRANCE TO IRVINE PARK
(Photograph by Hollywood Studios, Santa Ana)

SANTIAGO DAM AND RESERVOIR (IRVINE LAKE)

the property were getting out of hand; whisky and gambling played the devil with a trusted ranch employee; and the business of the properties "was being greatly neglected."

During the following year, the ranch problems grew worse instead of better. The early winter rainfall was so scant that many sheep and lambs died for lack of feed, and Irvine and Benjamin Flint closed their ranges to the flocks of Bixby and his partner Moore.

Grazing conditions improved in March, but the situation became so acute a few months later that all but ten or twelve thousand sheep were driven away to find new grazing lands in San Luis Obispo County or even farther north. Some sheep were also apparently held through the drought in the higher ranges of the Santa Ana Mountains.

The loss of sheep and the great reduction in the size of the flocks left on the home ranges led Irvine to urge every possible economy in ranch operations. "It's *very, very dear* cooking," he wrote to the new manager, when an examination of the payroll showed that two Chinese were employed at sixty dollars a month and board to cook for themselves and six other men, "and it is *one of the many leaks* that have constituted the enormous running expense of the ranch so that all the products of the property have not paid its bills."

Wages on the San Joaquin for June 1870 amounted to $723, which seemed to Irvine to represent a much higher rate than prevailed on the ordinary sheep ranch. He was anxious to know how many persons were "supported on the ranch," how many were in the sheep camps, how many worked in and about the house and what they did. Fifteen dollars a month seemed to him an adequate wage for the ordinary employee, and he breathed more freely when the Chinese cooks were gotten rid of. He hoped the ranch payroll could be reduced to $500 a month, but with thirty or forty employees this seemed impossible.

In those early days, and for many years thereafter, hobos, itinerant workers, and "bindle stiffs," all called by the generic name of tramps, roamed the southern California countryside in great numbers, especially in winter, and often made themselves a pest to large and small ranchers alike. According to Irvine, the Rancho San Joaquin supported never less than five of these gentry—far more than its share —and he urged the manager to devise some method of lessening the nuisance.

The manager himself was not altogether satisfactory and lost caste with Irvine (who had begun his career in California as a prospector) when he became excited over the prospect of finding gold on the ranch as the result of the wiles of an "old miner" who brought him some crudely doctored samples. When the manager sent Irvine a box of the salted specimens, accompanied by an optimistic letter, Irvine replied in disgust:

In reference to yours of the 4th inst. I hardly know what to say. This however I will say if any more "gold miners" want to send cobblestones here by express, let them do it at their own expense.

What kind of an opinion must the fellow have of you to attempt to palm off on you such a cheap and bare-faced swindle? Had you used a knife at once you would have discovered that the "Golden Fleece" was only ruble on the surface and for this purpose a cobblestone (showing you to be wholly uninitiated) was as good as any other. But under no other circumstances would such stones as you sent show any affinity for gold. If you want to see how it is done just take any piece of rock and rub hard the edge of a $20 piece upon it . . . and you will have equally as good specimens as any the "old miner" gave you. I only hope he has not succeeded in wheedling you out of any of your money.

As yet, apparently no attempt had been made to cultivate any part of the Irvine-Flint-Bixby ranches, but the property was used entirely for the pasturage of sheep; and when the manager asked permission to do a little farming on his own responsibility and at his own risk, Irvine gave guarded consent. "I have no objection to your farming all you want to do. It will not be a bit of expense to the ranch. Indeed I would like much to see a little farming done there but we must not add to current expenses which are already beyond endurance. You see I am a little afraid of the cost of the experiment."

Six months later, Irvine informed the manager that he was willing to have parts of the ranch devoted to tenant farming, but the tenants would have to assume all the risk and expense of the venture, and he would not advertise that the lands were for rent.

About this time, the Southern Pacific Railroad persuaded the government to bring suit to invalidate Irvine's title to the large area which the decision of the United States District Court had added to the original "4 square leagues, more or less," of the Rancho Lomas de Santiago, as described in Chapter V. The suit, if successful, would throw the lands in question into the public domain and thereby enable the railroad to obtain a highly desirable right of way across the tract and claim every alternate section along the right of way as a government grant.

The suit was brought in March 1876 in the United States Circuit Court of California. In it the government sought to have the court declare that "a certain Grant purporting to have been made to one Teodosio Yorba on the 26th day of May, 1846, by Pio Pico . . . [for] the Lomas de Santiago . . . was fraudulently issued and was invalid and ought not to have been confirmed." The government also prayed that the grant and confirmation should be set aside, the patent recalled and canceled, and the lands declared public lands of the United States. Benjamin Flint, Thomas Flint, Llewellyn Bixby, William T. Glassell, and James Irvine were named as defendants in the suit.

A memorandum of November 11, 1925, on the grant of the Lomas de Santiago, transmitted by the United States Attorney General to Hubert Work, Secretary of the Interior under President Coolidge, contained the following interesting details relative to this action:

A suit to cancel the patent issued to Teodosio Yorba was urged upon the Department of Justice on behalf of the Southern Pacific Railway Co. in 1875. The Washington attorneys for the owners of the Rancho Lomas de Santiago filed a brief in opposition to such action and were granted hearings thereon. The case was fully considered by Solicitor General Phillips who prepared an extensive memorandum, approved the bill, and recommended to the Attorney General that it be filed. The bill was prepared in the Department of Justice and referred to the Secretary of the Interior on February 8, 1876, and filing of the suit to cancel the patent was approved by that official. On March 5, 1876, telegraphic instructions to file the suit against Flint and others to vacate the patent were given by the Attorney General to the United States attorney in California, and the suit was filed on March 17, 1876. The matter was carefully considered in the Interior Department and the Commissioner of the General Land Office on October 23, 1875, made an extensive report to the Attorney General on the facts of the case as disclosed by official records.

The case of the United States *v.* Flint (1875-78) was heard by Justice Stephen J. Field and decided adversely to the government. In March 1878 the solicitor general asked J. M. Coghlan, the United States attorney in California, if there was any reason why the suit should not be dismissed and instructed him to "ascertain and report whether the Southern Pacific Railroad Co. had any further interest in the Flint case." S. W. Sanderson, attorney for the Southern Pacific Company, advised Coghlan that the railroad "was interested in the institution and prosecution of the Flint case [Rancho Lomas de Santiago], but upon its decision in the circuit court determined, so far as it was concerned, to prosecute the case no further. . . . While the Southern Pacific Railroad Co. would be benefited by a decision in favor of the United States it does not desire any further prosecution of the case."

On April 6, 1878, Coghlan thereupon wrote the Attorney General: "In relation to the inquiry as to whether the United States has any special interest in said case, and what I know, if anything, why the case may not be dismissed, I have to state that I am not aware that the Government has any special interest in said case, and know of no reason why the same should not be dismissed."

The appeal of the "Flint Case" was accordingly dismissed on motion of the solicitor general on April 22, 1878, and title to the Lomas de Santiago was not again challenged for a long generation.

By 1876 Irvine was ready to undertake the southern ranch venture solely on his own account and acquired his partners' interests in the Lomas de Santiago, the San Joaquin, and the fringe of the Santiago de Santa Ana, apparently paying $150,000 for his associates' holdings in the three properties.[1] Some time later he engaged Charles T. Healey to make a survey of the ranches.

[1] Irvine also bought a fifth undivided interest in the Lomas de Santiago, which had been acquired by two partners named Lowe and Steinhart, and a number of other smaller properties adjoining the larger ranches.

Irvine had scarcely acquired full ownership of the three properties before the historic drought of 1876-77 burned up the ranges, brought ruin and devastation to the grazing industry, and destroyed the sheep of southern California almost as effectually as a similar drought had destroyed the range cattle industry in the mid-sixties. Available records do not show to what extent Irvine's own flocks suffered from this disaster, but presumably his losses were comparable to those of other southern California sheep ranchers.

Uncertain boundaries and long-delayed court decisions encouraged squatters, as the large property owners styled them, or homesteaders, as the would-be settlers called themselves, to occupy parts of the properties, and Irvine's attorneys and ranch superintendent were kept busy dealing, in one way or another, with the trespassers.

Such disputes often furnished the basis for newspaper attacks upon the many large landholdings that still remained in southern California. The Santa Ana *Herald* took occasion to criticize the owner of the newly created Irvine Ranch, for example, for both evading his rightful taxes and failing to contribute to the settlement and prosperity of the county. An article in the issue of December 31, 1881, said in part:

The liveliest town in Southern California this winter is Santa Ana. . . . A new brick hotel has been built. . . . More business is transacted in Santa Ana than in any other town along the coast. The township contains the following tracts of land: The San Joaquin rancho of 48,833 acres; the Santiago de Santa Ana, 62,516 acres; Lomas de Santa Ana [sic], 48,226 acres; Canyon de Santa Ana, 13,326 acres. The Lomas and San Joaquin ranchos are as yet uninhabited except by herders and one home ranch-house. They reach clear across the county from the ocean to the San Bernardino line, twenty miles long and nine and a half miles wide.

We traveled through the rancho, the property of James Irvine of San Francisco, a distance of nearly twelve miles, during which we saw no house nor found any improvement. Of the San Joaquin rancho of 48,900 acres, one-third is level and well adapted to cultivation. There are three artesian wells on the tract, and the whole is susceptible of irrigation by artesian water. Mr. Irvine's adjoining rancho, the Lomas de Santiago, containing 47,000 acres, contains about 9,000 acres of fine wheat, corn, and fruit land, but is wholly uninhabited. . . . At present there are only about 35,000 head of sheep upon them, and it is estimated that one hundred thousand sheep could be fed there each year. This immense estate, so dreary and desolate, presents a vivid contrast to the adjoining rancho, which has been made to blossom like a rose in its beauty and luxuriance. The Santa Ana rancho, which was originally granted to the Yorba family, has been cut up and sold out into tracts upon which thousands of happy homes may now be found, including the towns of Santa Ana, Orange, and Tustin City, three of the prettiest and most prosperous places in California.

Perhaps in part because of such attacks Irvine, in 1882, undertook to subdivide and sell part of his share of the Rancho Santiago de Santa Ana and a portion of the Rancho San Joaquin. The land was divided into forty-acre farms, and a main highway a hundred and twenty feet wide and lateral roads sixty feet wide were constructed through the property. The land was sold on the installment plan, and the failure of some of the purchasers to complete the required payments resulted in considerable litigation.[2]

[2]In 1880 Irvine became involved in a long-drawn-out suit and cross suit with the McFadden brothers over the ownership of certain lands. The suit continued for at least five years.

To write the history of the four McFadden brothers—James, John, Robert, and Archie—and their descendants would be to write much of the history of the Santa Ana Valley. Arthur McFadden, son of Robert McFadden, is now a director of the Irvine Company and a trustee of the James Irvine Foundation.

Irvine's appearance in the role of subdivider followed a number of more or less successful undertakings of a similar nature in the Santa Ana Valley. The pioneer Anaheim Colony of 1857 was established on part of the Rancho San Juan Cajon de Santa Ana, but a number of later subdivisions were laid out on lands formerly included in the Rancho Santiago de Santa Ana.

As early as 1867 Columbus Tustin and N. A. Stafford bought some 1,300 acres of this ranch for $2,000. The tract, to use present-day names, was bounded on the north by First Street, on the east by Newport Road, on the south by McFadden Street, and on the west by Main Street of Santa Ana. In the subsequent division of the property between the two purchasers, Stafford took the west half and Tustin the east. Tustin at once laid out a town on the eastern boundary of his tract, "between Gospel Swamp and Tomato City," to which he gave the ambitious name of Tustin City.

In the early seventies, according to C. E. Utt, the "city" still consisted of "a big sounding name, a small store and blacksmith shop, with a few settlers' shacks hidden around in the thickets of wild mustard." One of the largest and oldest buildings in the little community was a square, unpainted, two-story structure at the corner of D and Main streets that had been designed originally to serve as a hotel but eventually became the home of the Utt family and the location of the well-known L. Utt's "Pioneer Store."

The subsequent development of Tustin was due in considerable measure to the patronage of its stores and the support of its interests by the owner, employees, and tenants of the Irvine Ranch and to Irvine's sale of land adjacent to the town for subdivision into residence and building lots.

In 1869, two years after the founding of Tustin, William H. Spurgeon, the "father of Santa Ana," bought another portion of the Rancho Santiago de Santa Ana, divided part of it into residence and business lots, and gave the name of ranch and river to the new town. Santa Ana of that day was bounded on the north by what is now Seventh Street, on the south by First Street, on the east by Spurgeon Street, and on the west by West Street, or Broadway. It is said that the site of the new settlement was covered by such a huge mustard forest that Spurgeon was forced to climb a sycamore tree to get a bird's-eye view of the land he proposed to purchase.[3]

As late as 1873, according to early residents of Santa Ana, the new town had neither "market, fruit nor vegetable stands, laundry nor hotel. . . . The valley irrigation system was in its infancy. Farmers were just beginning to plant trees and vines. Melons and vegetables had to take the place of fruit till the trees and vines began to bear." There were still no church buildings in Santa Ana; two lots on the corner of Second and Main streets sold for $150; lumber was brought all the way from sawmills in the San Bernardino Mountains; and mail came by semiweekly stage that ran between Los Angeles and San Diego.

The establishment of Santa Ana and Tustin City led to a major alteration in the route of the old Los Angeles–San Diego stage road—El Camino Viejo—that followed the base of the Santiago foothills across the Irvine Ranch. The new road ran through Santa Ana and Tustin, angled off to the southwest, and eventually ran almost parallel to the modern

[3]Sometime in the seventies, C. E. French became manager of the Rancho San Joaquin. The family lived "in the old San Joaquin Ranch house by the Laguna Hills." Mrs. French served, without pay, as the first librarian of Santa Ana. The Spurgeon family has remained important in Santa Ana affairs, and William H. Spurgeon, III, is now a vice-president of the Irvine Company.

United States Highway 101, but somewhat nearer the Laguna Hills.

In 1871, Andrew Glassell and Alfred Beck Chapman, members of one of the leading law firms in Los Angeles, laid out still another town, in the form of a square around a plaza, a few miles from the Irvine Ranch, and called it Richland. The Richland Farm District, a tract of six hundred acres surrounding the town, was surveyed and platted at the same time. The land was advertised as being "beautifully located, under the flow of the A. B. Chapman Canal . . . well watered, sheltered, and above the influence of frosts." The ranches ranged from ten to forty acres in size. The town of Richland is now known as Orange.

Life in the early towns—Anaheim, Tustin City, Santa Ana, Orange—no less than on the ranches, was semifrontier in character. The settlers had the advantage of roads, stores, and neighbors. They were not compelled to fight Indians or organized bands of outlaws. Doctors, schools, and churches were usually within easy reach. But most of the standard necessities of modern living were as yet unknown, and few even of those conveniences elsewhere in common use were available in the new communities. Certainly the housewife of that time, as the following description graphically attests, knew nothing of the laborsaving devices which her more fortunate (if often less happy) successor of today enjoys.

A galvanized iron tub or two (not stationary), a washboiler and a washboard comprised the paraphernalia for the laundry. With water hauled in barrels or dipped from the ditch there were no bathrooms; the same tubs served for bathing. An outhouse, built over a vault digged in the ground, was the toilet. Washstands with bowls and pitchers stood in the bedrooms. Usually there was a "washbench" outside the back door, with a basin and soap-dish for the use of the men when they came in from the fields. A broom, dust-pan and dustcloth, supplemented by a scrubbing-brush and pail, did all . . . that the vacuum-cleaner does now. There was no bakery, so the housewife baked her own bread. . . . She made her own butter, too. . . .

Water was carried in from outdoors and was carried out to be emptied. . . . People went to the cañon to pick up wood for the cooking-stove. Kerosene lamps were used for lighting.

The limitations of living conditions, just mentioned, were part of the normal experience of every newly developed region of that early day. Most settlers expected nothing else and accepted the discomforts and inconveniences imposed by their environment as they accepted Nature's unpleasant gifts of drought, floods, wind, and frost.

More serious than these occasional natural misfortunes just mentioned, and no more subject to control by the individual, were the lack of available markets, the ruinously low prices, and the prohibitive cost of transportation against which the farmers had to contend. "The more we raised," said one early settler, speaking of those ever-present evils, "the poorer we were likely to become. Indeed, all land-owners were poor."

The soil itself, however, was as rich as that of the land of Goshen. Corn grew so tall that a man could scarcely reach the lowest ear on the stalk with an ordinary walking stick, and production often ran as high as a hundred and twenty-five bushels an acre. A yield of two hundred and twenty-five sacks of potatoes an acre and pumpkins that weighed two hundred pounds and more were not uncommon.

The country, too, was a hunter's paradise, and in many households wild game was often the most important item, with the exception of bread, in the family diet. Deer were particularly abundant in the Santa Ana Mountains. A few antelope could be found in the foothills or on the nearby plains. Rabbits and quail were so numerous as to constitute major pests. Great flocks of geese ate up the farmers' grain and often covered the ground, literally, by the uncounted thousands, especially near what is now the center of Tustin.

Market hunters shipped ducks, geese, and quail out of the valley by the thousands. Grizzly and black bear, gray wolves, wildcats, and mountain lion were to be found in great numbers in the mountains and cañons. Hundreds of coyotes ranged over plain and hill and took heavy toll of the flocks of sheep. Rattlesnakes were so numerous that farmers in badly infested areas had to wrap sacking about the hooves of their horses to keep the latter from being killed.

"Hawks, of many kinds and sizes, sailed above the plain, and tireless buzzards circled, circled, in graceful dignity," wrote Mrs. Margaret Gardner of the early development of the community of Orange.

Far up, an occasional eagle screamed, for they lived in the cañons then, to the annoyance of the sheep men.

It may be, too, that one saw huge condors sailing above the hills, for there were some in the Santa Ana Mountains. Mr. Pleasants tells me that he saw one, killed where the County Park is (in the lower Santiago Cañon), that measured thirteen feet from wing-tip to wing-tip. . . .

Cactus birds built inaccessible nests in the center of cactus clumps, and butcher birds left grewsome records of their activities in the dried and shriveled bodies of mice, chipmunks, large insects and small birds impaled on thorns or, later on barbed wire. . . .

I have omitted mention of the tarantulas, scorpions, centipedes, trap-door spiders, gophers, foxes, king-snakes, gopher-snakes, blue-racers, red-racers, man-faced owls, cat-owls, screech-owls, blue-jays, skunks, wood-peckers.

As early as 1865, a small steamer called the *Vaquero* paid regular visits to Newport Bay, chiefly to collect hides, meat, and tallow from the nearby ranchos. In 1873 the well-known brothers—James, Robert, and John McFadden—already owners of some four or five thousand acres formerly belonging to the Rancho Santiago de Santa Ana, bought a small dock and warehouse that had been built a few months before on a site below the bluff or palisades at the dividing line between Upper and Lower Newport Bay, northwest of Linda Isle, and began importing lumber on a large scale (at least for those pioneer days) and shipping out grain, wool, and a few other agricultural products.

The McFaddens called the prosperous new shipping center Newport and helped to construct a good road for the shipment of freight to Santa Ana.[4] In 1888, to overcome the difficulty of entering and navigating the winding bay, the brothers erected a pier, on the site of the present Newport pier, running some 1,200 feet from shore, and in 1892 laid out the town of Newport as a beach resort. Like the Irvine Company in later years, the McFaddens leased rather than sold lots in the new town. The first hotel in the beach resort was built in 1893.

With the completion of the pier at Newport, the McFaddens undertook to build a railroad from Santa Ana to the harbor; but the line was not actually completed until 1892. Thereafter it is said that between five and six hundred cargoes were handled over the Newport pier during the course of a single year. As business increased, the Southern Pacific Railroad sought to acquire both pier and rail-

[4]The town was later, for a time, called Port Orange.

road, but the McFaddens, thanks to a long-standing feud with the Southern Pacific, refused to sell, and it was not until 1899 that the Huntington interests, by using a dummy purchaser, obtained the properties. Newport's day as a shipping center, however, was then almost over, and a few years later commercial shipping was abandoned.

9

END OF THE FIRST GENERATION

By the mid-eighties, the semifrontier conditions described in the last chapter were rapidly giving way in the Santa Ana Valley, as elsewhere in southern California, to a more advanced social and economic order. The completion of the Southern Pacific railroad to Los Angeles in 1876 and the coming of the Santa Fe nine years later changed the agricultural outlook for the Los Angeles–Santa Ana basins, brought about a large influx of population, stimulated the subdivision of many large landholdings, and ushered in the "Great Boom" of 1886-88.

But the founder of the Irvine Ranch was not permitted to participate to any great degree in these new developments. James Irvine died in San Francisco on March 15, 1886.

Irvine's heirs-at-law were his eighteen-year-old son, James, and his wife, Margaret.[1] He left few debts and no community property.

His will, dated June 6, 1885, was filed for probate in San Francisco on April 6, 1886. In it Irvine provided that certain relatives and friends should serve as executors and devisees in trust for his only son. The list included Irvine's wife; his brother, George; his brother-in-law, James W.

---

[1] James Irvine was twice married. His first wife died in 1874. Some years later Irvine married Margaret Byrne.

Byrne; his attorney, Edwin B. Mastick; Isaac E. Davis; and George Moffatt.

Out of his estate, Irvine directed that cash bequests, in the amount of over $100,000, should be provided by the sale of real estate for his wife, brothers, sisters, and other relatives. His wife and each of seven other beneficiaries were also to receive substantial gifts of land (none of which, however, should run above $5,000 in value) out of his southern California holdings.[2]

A tract of 2,880 acres, lying partly in the Santiago de Santa Ana and partly in the San Joaquin, was specifically allocated to James Irvine, Jr. The latter was also to inherit the rest of his father's estate when he reached the age of twenty-five. Until that time, however, after carrying out the other provisions of the will, the trustees were given authority to lease, improve, or sell the assets of the estate at their discretion. A clause in the will also provided that if the Los Angeles County ranches were sold for more than $1,200,000, the beneficiaries previously mentioned should receive twice the amount of the specified cash bequests.

The official inventory and appraisal of the Irvine estate was filed with the court on September 30, 1886. At that time the estate consisted of real property in Los Angeles County, valued at $748,500; personal property in Los Angeles County, valued at $61,629.23; real property elsewhere in California, valued at $431,380.75; and personal property elsewhere in California, valued at $41,671.03. The total value of the estate was thus $1,283,181.01.

In the description of the Irvine property situated in Los

[2]Mrs. Irvine also received a substantial life income and a life estate in a house in San Francisco that the executors were instructed to build and furnish with funds from the estate.

THE IRVINE HOME, BUILT ON THE RANCH IN 1900
(*Photograph by Jim England Photography, Los Angeles*)

THE IRVINE COMPANY HEADQUARTERS
(Photograph by Jim England Photography, Los Angeles)

Angeles County, the area of the Rancho Lomas de Santiago was given as 47,226 acres (less three relatively small parcels) and its value placed at $222,000; Rancho San Joaquin contained 48,803 acres (less several hundred acres that had been subdivided and sold) and was valued at $408,000; no figure was given for the extent of the estate's holdings in the Rancho Santiago de Santa Ana, but they were appraised at $118,500. These three parcels, now the Irvine Ranch, thus had an area of well over 100,000 acres and an appraised value of $748,500. Livestock on the three ranches was valued at about $54,000, and a fifth interest in crops of barley on 500 acres, grown "on a tenant sharing basis," was estimated at $800.

In due time, the distribution of land was made to Margaret Irvine and the other beneficiaries under the will. The trustees also made numerous efforts to dispose of the southern California ranches, as James Irvine apparently expected them to do; and on one occasion, only a split-second's delay in the bidding prevented the sale of all the Irvine holdings at public auction and presumably the subdivision of most of the farming land now included in the great ranch. The circumstances were as follows:

On April 16, 1887, the trustees "offered and agreed to sell" at least 100,000 acres of the Irvine ranches in Los Angeles County at public auction. The sale was held at the office of John D. Bicknell and Stephen M. White, well-known attorneys of Los Angeles, on July 16, 1887. Before the bidding started, it was agreed that the land should go to the highest bidder; that no bid of less than $1,300,000 would be accepted; that a certified check for $50,000, to be forfeited if the balance of the purchase price were not completed within sixty days, must accompany the successful bid; that the trustees, upon request, would lend the purchaser up to a maximum of $900,000 to be applied on the payment; and finally, by agreement among the possible purchasers, that all bids must be made within thirty minutes from the actual start of the sale.

The auction was duly held at the announced time and place in the presence of three trustees—George Irvine, E. B. Mastick, and J. W. Byrne. The two major competitors for the land, acting either for themselves or for their principals, were W. D. Smith and A. E. Davis. In the hectic closing moments of the sale J. D. Bicknell, the official timekeeper, became momentarily confused and designated first Davis and then Smith as the successful bidder.

On July 20, 1887, Davis filed suit in the Superior Court of Los Angeles County, first, to restrain the trustees of the Irvine estate from deeding the land to Smith and, second, to compel them to convey the land to him as soon as he paid the deferred balance of his final bid. The court's summary of the case and final decision were as follows:

That several bids above $1,300,000 were made and at the expiration of said time said Smith bid $1,380,000. Whereupon said Bicknell called time. Immediately thereupon as soon as the same could be spoken plaintiff bid $1,385,000 and said Bicknell addressing plaintiff said "You have it." Supposing the bid of $1,380,000 came from plaintiff, while as a fact it came from said Smith.

That thereupon plaintiff placed upon the table in front of said Bicknell a certified check for $50,000 drawn by J. G. Fair upon the Bank of California payable to his own order and endorsed by him to plaintiff and by plaintiff to E. B. Mastick; and said Smith placed on the table before said Bicknell, a check for $50,000 drawn by George H. Bonebrake, Cashier of the Los Angeles National Bank. . . . said trustees refused to accept said check and award the sale to either plaintiff or defendant Smith.

. . . The Court is of the opinion that neither plaintiff nor defendant Smith is entitled to the decree prayed for or to any relief and orders judgment accordingly.

In this dramatic fashion the difference of a second's time, a little more or less, determined the fate of the Irvine Ranch!

Though in this instance the trustees refused to accept the offer of either Smith or Davis, they soon renewed their efforts to sell the Los Angeles properties, either as a whole or in separate parcels. Potential buyers were found in San Francisco, St. Louis, New York, and elsewhere, and from time to time the southern California newspapers reported that the ranches had been or were about to be disposed of.[3]

The most important of such stories appeared early in August 1888, when both the Los Angeles *Times* and the Santa Ana *Blade* announced that a hundred thousand acres in Los Angeles County had been sold for $1,500,000. The Los Angeles *Times* characterized the (supposed) transaction as probably the largest sale in the history of the county and closed in the typical booster style, "This is 'business.'"

A year later George Whidden, the manager of the ranch, wrote to James Irvine, "Lyons has a contract with Governor Watterman (in his own hand writing) for that mine in Julian for two million dollars. Now that Lyons has sold it for three million the governor refuses to allow him the difference. This amount Lyons was going to place on the purchase of the San Joaquin so there may be a chance for a sale of the ranch to him yet."

The rumor of the sale of the Irvine properties and the uncertainty as to their future kept the neighboring com-

[3] James Phelan, afterward senator from California and one of the financial backers of the famous Ruef-Schmitz graft investigations in San Francisco, was one of the most likely prospects and spent some time visiting and inspecting the ranch.

munities of Santa Ana, Orange, and Tustin more or less on tenterhooks and made it difficult for the manager to know what crops (if any) to plant, what leases (if any) to negotiate, what plans (if any) to make relative to the sheep and cattle on the ranch. For the most part, however, these problems were dealt with as though no change in ownership was contemplated, and the ranch continued its gradual transition from a pastoral to a diversified agricultural economy.

In the meantime the trustees became involved in difficulties with the Southern Pacific and Santa Fe railroads, both of which had to build across the ranch to reach San Diego.

A branch line of the Southern Pacific had been extended from Los Angeles to Anaheim as early as 1875. The people of the Santa Ana Valley were overjoyed at the coming of the railroad, for it promised enhanced land values, markets for their products, and an end to isolation. "With this system in operation," wrote the exultant editor of the Anaheim *Gazette*, "there is assured a paradise of wealth and refinement in Southern California. All praise to God, Who, after years of frowning, smiled upon our land with an exceedingly gracious smile."

Two years later the line was extended to Santa Ana. The Southern Pacific subsequently attempted to obtain a right of way through the Irvine Ranch with the ultimate object of reaching San Diego. When the effort failed, the company held its proposed line to San Diego in abeyance until the coming of the Santa Fe ten years later precipitated a major struggle between the two rivals for freight and passenger business throughout southern California.

At that time a railroad not infrequently obtained a desired right of way by the simple expedient of laying its tracks without the owner's permission—and often in the face of his express opposition—and afterward preventing him both by force and legal action from removing the rails.

In attempting to extend its line beyond Tustin in 1887, the Southern Pacific resorted to this method. One Saturday afternoon, after the closing of the Los Angeles courts for the weekend holiday made it impossible for the owners of the affected property to obtain an injunction in time to stop the company's action, the railroad's construction crew began to build an improvised line through Tustin and on across the Irvine Ranch. If the strategy had succeeded, the citizens and ranchers might have whistled to the wind so far as getting the tracks removed was concerned; but a group of landowners, armed with rifles and shotguns, stopped the construction work and drove the crew off the disputed right of way. This action ended the Southern Pacific's attempt to build down the coast across the Irvine properties.

Meanwhile, the Santa Fe was also seeking a right of way across the Irvine Ranch over which it could extend its line from Santa Ana to San Juan Capistrano and so on down the coast to San Diego. Accordingly, on February 14, 1887, the San Bernardino and San Diego Railroad, a subsidiary of the Santa Fe, filed suit in the Superior Court of Los Angeles County against the Irvine trustees "to condemn to the public use of plaintiff for its right of way upon which to build a Railroad and for plaintiff's main tracks, side tracks, turnouts, switches and for such other purposes as are necessary and incident to railroad construction, maintenance, and operation." The desired right of way was a hundred feet in width, extended across the Rancho San Joaquin, and contained approximately 109.34 acres.

The case was never brought to trial. Instead, on April

25, 1887, the Irvine trustees deeded to the San Bernardino and San Diego Railroad the right of way prayed for in the suit, and added to it a generous site for a depot, side tracks, and warehouse.

The deeds to the right of way and depot site were conditioned upon the payment of $4,500 by the railroad to the owners, the erection within six months of "a first class regular station for freight and passengers," the construction of a fence on both sides of the right of way, permission on the part of the railway for its line to be intersected or crossed by other railways, roads, highways, irrigation ditches, and the like as prescribed by the owners of the Irvine Ranch, and certain other minor provisions.

This friendly settlement of the issue of the right of way marked the beginning of an amicable relationship between the Irvine Ranch and the Santa Fe railroad that has continued with few interruptions down to the present time.

In addition to the right-of-way problems, the trustees also faced a potential controversy over a disputed boundary line between the Rancho San Joaquin and its immediate neighbor to the southeast, the Rancho Cañada de Los Alisos. This difficulty was amicably settled in 1887 when the Irvine trustees quitclaimed some of the disputed land to Dwight Whiting, owner of Los Alisos, and he in turn quitclaimed other land to the Irvine estate.

In March 1889, after long and persistent agitation, the large, unwieldy county of Los Angeles was divided, and the portion lying south and east of a line drawn approximately along the course of Coyote Creek was formed into the present Orange County. The Irvine Ranch, whose area was certified to the State Board of Equalization as 105,000 acres, occupied approximately a third of the new county.

In the spring of that year a number of the ranch employees joined a mining stampede to Lower California that had aroused some excitement from Los Angeles to San Diego. "A good many idle men went to the mines from this section," wrote Whidden. "So far we have not heard from them and do not know what success they had there. The old stage coach that ran from Santa Ana to San Juan was brought into use to take a party from the ranch to the new mining camp. Buckboards and other kinds of conveyances were sent out on the road loaded down with supplies and articles necessary for a mining outfit. Many that have gone with great expectations will return soon, having had an experience but with less money than they started with."

Sheep raising continued an important business on the ranch long after the first James Irvine's death, but by 1888 the large flocks of earlier years had dwindled to eleven or twelve thousand head, and the spring clip of that year yielded only about 60,000 pounds of wool. Seventy men, mostly Indians, were employed for the shearing. The price of wool was low, and the Irvine trustees sold four thousand ewes to Crommery and Hall, lessees of a portion of the San Joaquin Ranch, for $2.80 a head. In addition to sheep, the Irvine Ranch also ran a substantial number of cattle and leased much of the range at sixty-two and a half cents an acre to outsiders.

By the late eighties, however, the Irvine Ranch was fast undergoing the radical transition from a grazing and pastoral stage to a farming economy that characterized the general agricultural development of most of southern California.

In the light of later developments, the agricultural experiments of the eighties and nineties on the ranch have special interest. At the close of 1888, more than 5,000 acres of the Irvine properties had been leased, in relatively small tracts, for raising hay and grain, and many additional tenants were expected as soon as the new policy of the ranch became more widely known. The average cash rental for such leases was approximately three dollars an acre, but most of the land was farmed on shares.

In addition to grain farming, more and more land was being put under cultivation. A small vineyard was set out, chiefly for home use, but the destruction of the once flourishing raisin-grape industry in the Santa Ana Valley by the devastating blight of 1886 discouraged any attempt to develop viticulture on the Irvine Ranch on a large scale.

The trustees made a stong effort, however, to establish the olive industry as one of the major interests of the ranch. George Whidden, the ranch manager, planted an olive nursery in 1889, using for the most part cuttings of Mission olive trees, a variety noted for its oil-producing qualities, that he obtained from the Forster trees at San Juan Capistrano. When the nursery stock was sufficiently mature, Whidden planted a tract of a hundred and sixty acres, not far from the present ranch headquarters. A few of these trees are still living, but years of effort and costly experimentation eventually showed that the Irvine Ranch, primarily because of its proximity to the coast, was not well adapted to successful olive culture.

A walnut orchard, irrigated at first by tank wagon, was also set out sometime in the early nineties, and over 11,000 eucalyptus, or "gum," trees, supplied by a dealer in Anaheim, were planted for both wood and windbreaks. A few orange trees were also set out, but at that early date the fruit was used only for home consumption.

Two foxhounds were added to the ranch ménage, both to keep jack rabbits under control and to furnish a new element of sport. The hounds were "very industrious and did a good deal of hunting on their own account"; but after about a month the rabbits were able to live again at peace. Both hounds suddenly died, probably of poison.

In December 1889 "the heavens broke loose," as the Santa Ana *Weekly Blade* exclaimed, and long-continued rains caused serious floods in many parts of southern California. The Los Angeles, San Gabriel, and Santa Ana rivers went on a wild rampage. Bridges, railroad tracks, houses, and farm lands were washed away. The Santa Fe railroad tracks on the Mojave Desert and its branch line through Temecula Cañon were rendered useless. Part of Santa Ana was under four feet of water, and the town was without train service for over a week.

"There was a heavy rain during the greater part of last night," said the Los Angeles *Times* of December 24.

The Santa Ana River and Santiago Creek are out of their banks, the former flooding the Newport district, west and south of the city, causing great loss of crops and other property. The latter has changed its course into the old channel east of the city, and is flowing through the heart of the San Joaquin ranch.

The bridges are gone on the California Southern and Southern Pacific between Santa Ana and Los Angeles.

There have been no trains between here and San Diego since yesterday.

The floods did only minor damage to the Irvine Ranch; but the rains aggravated, curiously enough, the perennial squatter problem with which the trustees had to deal.

"A number of parties, six in all," wrote Whidden to Mastick, have gone onto the Newport Mesa today and have located there as squatters. I have telegraphed to Mr. Irvine in Los Angeles to return here. This may be difficult owing to the conditions of the roads as we have been cut off from all communication for several days. I expect to hear from him tomorrow. One party went on there from the Bolsa last week with a lot of cattle and I had the tenant commence proceedings against him for trespass. The constable took possession of some horses belonging to him. The suit will probably come to trial in a day or two. Some action should be taken in this matter immediately otherwise all of the mesa will be occupied by these squatters.

Owing to high water around Newport, these parties are obliged to vacate from there and having the idea that the San Joaquin has more land than belongs to it they come here to make the fight. It is presumed by some that there is a league back of this movement of the squatters. Mr. McFadden seems to be greatly interested in this matter in our behalf and says that a fence should have been run along the line even if it were only one wire so that it would have been an enclosure. It would have prevented this trouble.

By 1890 the trouble with the squatters had subsided, but the Irvine trustees soon became involved in a dispute over the question of a right of way across the ranch for a line of the Postal Telegraph Company to San Diego. The controversy was somewhat similar to that in which the Southern Pacific Railroad Company was concerned three years earlier and involved injunctions, lawsuits, and more than one successful attack on the telegraph company's offending poles by ranch ax brigade.

Those familiar with the size of the Irvine Ranch and its sprawling reach from the mountains to the sea—an effective barrier to any unauthorized right of way to San Diego —found a touch of humor in the instructions sent from the Eastern headquarters of the Postal Telegraph Company to its local representatives—"If you can't build through the ranch, go around it."

About the time of the first James Irvine's death, the Santiago Cañon became the scene of one of the most unusual examples of gracious living that California has ever known.

Around Santiago Cañon itself centers much of the tradition, romance, and history of Orange County. The region was the scene of the Flores-Daniel episode and of numerous other, if lesser known, incidents of similar character. One of its branch cañons is called Limestone because here a pioneer resident of the sixties, Sam Shrewsbury, built the first kiln in Orange County. Another branch, Cañon de la Horca, as the Spaniards called it, was named Frémont Cañon by the Americans because of the repeated reference to his famous commander by a garrulous settler in the Santiago who once campaigned with John C. Frémont.

Cañon de la Madera originally provided pine logs for the adobes of the Californians, but the discovery of a coal deposit and later of silver-bearing ore led to a prospectors' stampede and the development of a vigorous if short-lived camp whose name, Silverado, still testifies to the feverish mining activities of the early seventies.

In the cañon of the Santiago, Madame Helena Modjeska, one of the most distinguished actresses in the history of the European or American stage, established her secluded but always hospitable home. The story of the Modjeska adventure is too familiar to require repetition in elaborate detail.[4] Impelled to leave Poland by personal sorrow and the unhappy state of her beloved country, the great actress, her husband (Count Bozenta), her fourteen-year-old son, and

[4]See Robert V. Hine, *California's Utopian Colonies* (San Marino, Calif., 1953), pp. 137-140.

a few other voluntary exiles—most distinguished of whom was Henryk Sienkiewicz, later the author of *Quo Vadis*—came to southern California in the seventies and for a time farmed unsuccessfully in the German colony at Anaheim.

During their stay at Anaheim, the Modjeskas visited Santiago Cañon and became willing captives of its beauty and solitude. At that time J. E. Pleasants, one of the most colorful figures in the Santa Ana basin, owned a small home a short distance above the mouth of Silverado Cañon, and there the Modjeskas frequently visited the pioneer settler and his wife.

In 1888, Madame Modjeska bought the Pleasants ranch, planted it luxuriantly to trees and shrubs, built a large and comfortable house, and named the whole the "Forest of Arden." The "Modjeska Ranch," as the property was commonly called, became known for its open-handed hospitality throughout the valley. The famous actress and her husband were simple, deeply religious people, and the neighboring ranchers welcomed them as friends. The fact that James Irvine, Jr., named his only daughter Kathryn Helena is evidence of that friendship.

10

DIVERSIFICATION

In 1892, James Irvine, Jr., married Frances Anita Plum of San Francisco. Three children were born of the union—James, Kathryn Helena, and Myford.

The year following his marriage, Irvine came into full possession of the great ranch his father had begun to acquire nearly thirty years before. He was to retain complete control and direction of the ranch until his death well over half a century later. On June 4, 1894, he incorporated his large holdings as "The Irvine Company" under the laws of the state of West Virginia.

During the first ten years of the younger Irvine's administration, the ranch continued its evolution from a pastoral to a farming stage, but its development was confined to field crops such as corn, potatoes, wheat, and especially beans and barley, rather than garden vegetables or orchards.

In 1895, over thirty-one thousand acres of the ranch were planted to barley, an area far larger than that devoted to all other crops combined. Part of the barley, known by the name of Chevalier, was raised for brewing purposes and shipped from Newport Landing to Port Costa on San Francisco Bay for export to Europe. In 1896, ordinary feed barley sold for fifty-seven and a half cents a hundredweight, while the "Chevalier" variety brought seventy cents. The average yield during that year was between eight and nine sacks an acre.

By the middle nineties, bean farming had become, next to the production of barley, the most important of ranch activities. In the fall of 1896, eighteen hundred acres were reserved for beans and leased to tenant farmers. Most of the latter came from Ventura County (where the bean industry had been established some years before), and in many cases the new tenants were offered special inducements to transfer their activities to the Irvine Ranch.

Under the usual Irvine practice, the tenant supplied the seed and farmed the land on a share-crop basis. The ranch advanced money to its tenants on notes bearing interest at ten per cent per annum and carried trustworthy tenants, if there was need, from one season to the next.

Leases were made only on an annual basis, and their renewal depended on the desirability of the tenant as a person and his ability as a farmer. Many of the tenants, however, remained on the ranch year after year, and son frequently succeeded father. The company's method of dealing with an unsatisfactory or inefficient tenant is well illustrated by the following letter:

We have spoken to you several times requesting you to immediately remove the castor beans and so-called wild tobacco which washed down from the canyon upon the land you are farming and which you have allowed to grow. Both of these plants are objectionable and practically destroy the ground if allowed to grow and spread. You could easily have plowed them up or mowed them if you had acted at the proper time. The noxious weeds are in a location to have their seeds spread over a large portion of the ranch by next winter's rain and some of the tenants have already complained in anticipation of this condition happening. We drove to your place the other day and found a man who had grubbed out some and was at work on others but he said he was not instructed to clean them all up. We wish to give you notice herein that unless you immediately clean them off the land and pile them where they can be burned later and the seed destroyed we will take action under clauses 11 and 12 of your lease and have them eradicated and will exercise the right under such clause of any portion of our lease to recover whatever expense we may incur in eradicating these noxious weeds. We regret to have to take this action but we have spoken to you and your brother several times and if you are indifferent in the matter we must protect our land and our tenants. We trust you will give this matter your immediate attention so that we will not be compelled to enforce our lease.

Ground squirrels caused heavy losses to the barley and bean crops alike, and on certain days the tenants and the ranch employees joined forces in a general poisoning crusade. Scale constituted another serious pest for the olive and other orchards and was sprayed with a solution of caustic soda, resin, and fish oil under a hundred and twenty pounds' pressure. Cattle rustlers made occasional raids on the stock of the larger ranches, and Irvine took the lead in persuading the various owners to co-operate in the arrest and prosecution of the thieves.

From 1896 to 1900, with the exception of the year 1897, southern California passed through another severe drought, the barley and bean crops on the Irvine Ranch suffered great damage, and its grazing lands were unable to carry anything like the normal number of cattle and sheep. Some of the cattle were sent to a range at Soda Lake in the Mojave Desert, about sixty miles from the mining camp of Daggett;

but the grass and water of that oasis soon gave out, and the cattle had to be shipped to another locality by rail.

The prolonged drought and the rapid expansion of crops dependent upon irrigation led Irvine to take more and more interest in the water supply and finally to drill twelve or fourteen additional wells to meet the needs of the ranch. Since the underground storage basin of the Santa Ana Valley had not then been drawn upon in any appreciable degree and the underground water level was still high, the wells furnished at least a temporary answer to the problem of irrigation.[1]

In 1897, Irvine donated a beautifully wooded tract of a hundred and sixty acres at the mouth of Santiago Cañon to the people of Orange County. The place had been a favorite picnic ground for nearby settlers and townspeople since the days of the early settlers, and under the name of Irvine Park the site continues to serve thousands of grateful visitors each year. In 1957 the company increased the park donation by another twenty acres.

Between 1900 and 1905, affairs on the ranch followed what might be called a fairly normal trend. Barley and beans (both lima and black-eyed), largely farmed on shares, continued to be the chief crops both in acreage and value. The annual walnut crop, harvested at times by Japanese labor, came to about twenty-two tons. Several thousand soft-shell walnut trees, some of which came from the ranch nursery, were planted during the season of 1905-06, and substantial progress was also made in raising alfalfa.

About that time Orange County became the center of

---

[1] The wells were first pumped with gasoline engines, but in 1913 the company began to obtain electric power from the Southern California Edison Company, and in the course of time all of its wells were pumped by electricity.

AERIAL VIEWS OF NEWPORT BAY, 1936 AND 1961
*(Photographs by Spence Air Photos, Los Angeles,
and Garth Chandler, Costa Mesa)*

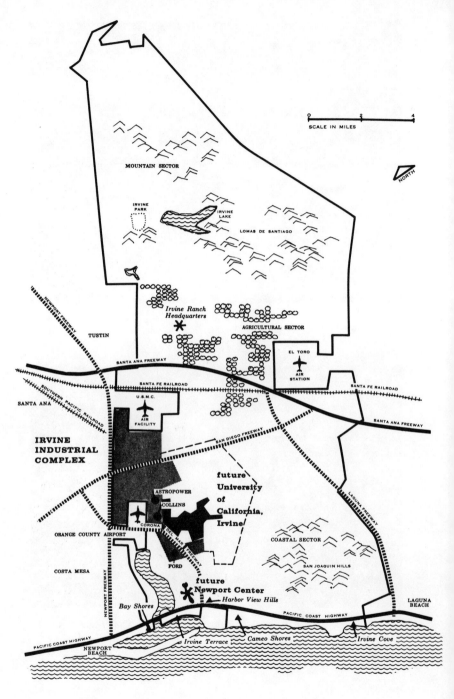

THE IRVINE RANCH, JANUARY 1961

celery production in southern California and annually shipped approximately seven or eight hundred cars to markets throughout the United States. The Irvine Ranch contributed to some extent to this production and in a few years added rhubarb and artichokes to its vegetable crops. In 1907, the peanut crop was valued at $12,000, and the same year a few acres were planted to flax.

In 1905, the California Canners Association leased between two and five hundred acres for the production of canning peas. Neither the terms of the lease nor the results of the venture are now known. A few months after the lease went into effect, however, Irvine complained that the association left the land uncultivated and so permitted a dense growth of mustard and malva to exhaust the moisture in the soil.

In spite of scale and occasional losses from other sources, the hundred-and-sixty-acre olive grove had an average yield of around a hundred thousand pounds a year. Irvine found it difficult to develop a market for the crop, however, and on at least one occasion complained of the plight of the unfortunate California olive growers to the federal government. Irvine's letter, written in 1907, was addressed to the "Chief of the General Appraisers" of the United States Customs, New York, and said in part:

The fact has just been brought to my attention of your having recently made a ruling admitting to this country, free of duty, black or ripe olives in brine in barrels.

As you probably know, California is the only state . . . producing olives on a commercial basis. The olive business here has had a most precarious existence owing to the fierce competition of sesame, peanut, cottonseed and cheap inferior olive oils admitted free of duty for manufacturing purposes, all of which find their way to a greater or less extent in making adulterated or inferior olive oil, against which it is simply impossible to compete with the pure California olive oil.

The result has been so disastrous that many olive orchards in the state have been up-rooted and none have been set out for many years past.

It requires seven to ten years to bring an orchard into good bearing.

Myself having a 160 acre orchard, and others, driven to desperation, made many experiments in preserving the ripe olive which had always been a failure and at last secured a canning process by which they can be put up and kept in good condition till used. By hard work we have built up what appears a prosperous business in these goods and rely upon them for our profit, making oil only out of olives over-ripe or too small to pickle, out of which we have been obtaining very little over cost, relying almost entirely on the pickles for profit.

With the passage of the pure food law, the oil business has assumed a much brighter outlook and it seems a hard blow right on top of that to have our ripe pickles brought under the ban of foreign competition.

The pickle business has been the salvation of the California olive grower.

Myself and others under the incorporated name of the "American Olive Company" have put about $140,000. into the plant and business and in the past four years have increased the selling price to the grower from $20 to $30 per ton to $40 for oil olives and $60 to $100 for pickles, in other words have raised them from a starvation price to a fair paying basis. California can and eventually will produce most of the olive oil and pickled olives consumed in the United States if given an opportunity and proper protection.

The manufacturing interests of the East, almost without exception get ample protection and it does seem a pity that this infant industry should not have its share.

I sincerely hope you will reconsider your ruling and if there is any possible way under the law, you will make a different ruling regarding ripe olives. They should have protection to the extent of at least 25 cents per gallon.

In this matter I am not speaking for myself alone, but for the olive growers of California in general as I know too well the true situation.

During this period, the ranch suffered no major misfortune; but from time to time the manager reported such minor ills as freezing temperatures (26° Fahrenheit), the "fiercest Santa Ana winds" in his experience,[2] difficulty in getting desirable tenants, persistent poaching by hunters, high charges for threshing, and lawsuits of various kinds.

In comparison with prices of the present day, those of most ranch products were then strikingly low. Barley brought from seventy-five cents to a dollar a sack, walnuts from nine to thirteen cents a pound, and black-eyed beans two and a half or three cents a pound; alfalfa hay averaged around seven dollars a ton; steers sold for three or three and a half cents a pound on the hoof; pasturage for horses and mules rented for a dollar or a dollar and a half a month per head; and sheep manure sold for a dollar a ton.

Wages were correspondingly low. A permanent ranch hand received about $28.00 a month and board; a vaquero, who furnished his own saddle and blankets, $30.00; a blacksmith $50.00; and a cattle foreman $75.00, without board. It was difficult to find—and keep—a man who was expected to cook for eighteen employees and six members of the Irvine family at $40.00 a month "and bring his own blankets," and the manager of the ranch was frequently engaged in a search for such a genius. As the ranch developed and assumed more and more the proportions of a large and complicated business, the problem of obtaining adequate office assistance and ranch supervision became an even more difficult problem for the manager. Beginning in the late nineties,

[2]December 9, 1905.

the latter position was filled for over twenty years by Irvine's brother-in-law, C. F. Krauss.

In 1902, Irvine apparently revived the idea of selling the ranch, or at least a large part of it, and wrote J. A. Turner of Santa Ana: "In reply to your request I herein state that at any time during the next six months should you produce any person or people to or through whom I might make a sale of the ranch or any portion thereof I will allow you a commission of 4% provided I am not called upon to pay a commission to anyone else. You will understand herein that this is not an option in any sense of the word nor will you be entitled to any commission unless the sale is absolutely completed and the money is paid." Four years later, by which time "one or two small corners of 1,000 and 2,000 acres" had been disposed of, Irvine had definitely abandoned all thought of selling the ranch as a whole.

Land values of that long-past generation were comparable to wages and farm prices. Irvine offered an undeveloped tract of 350 acres at Laguna for $125 an acre.[3] The Townsend-Dayman Investment Company of Long Beach bought 400 acres at Newport from the Irvine Company for $200 an acre and 1,280 acres less favorably situated at $100 an acre. The purchase included 20 acres of water-bearing lands. In 1904, George E. Hart acquired the site now known as Corona del Mar.

In February 1907 the manager of the Irvine Company wrote as follows to a prospective buyer:

We have about five miles around Newport Bay where we have made some sales in addition to about ten miles of direct ocean front. We have some land on either side of the bay which we would sell,

[3]In 1906, the Irvine Company advertised its willingness to lease 2,000 acres for quail and dove hunting at $600 a year.

and would probably be willing to sell from a mile to a mile and a half on the ocean front somewhere between the Bay and Laguna. The sales we have made east of the Bay have only run back half a mile more or less. The mile would face toward the ocean but carry you on pretty high ground. If you would take in the mile the price would be somewhat less than the half mile.

A Company is being formed to give all this land a good water supply, the water to be obtained and developed in the artesian belt at the head of the Bay. We would not care to sell all of our holdings at any price you could afford to pay. The land would range from $200 to $250 per acre. We would expect from a third to a half down on any sale and would prefer leaving the remainder stand on a mortgage or some form of security.

Much of the ranch continued to be farmed under the system of tenant leases introduced, though on a very small scale, by the first owner of the ranch. The Irvine Company no longer advanced money for teams, seed, or implements but received, in return, a smaller share of the crop. Leases were still made on a year-to-year basis.

The ranch sold large quantities of bean straw to orchards in the Redlands district and always used bean straw and stable manure instead of commercial fertilizer on its own large citrus groves. Ten thousand small sugar gums and as many gray gum trees were planted annually on the barren hillsides, both to furnish wood and to conserve water.

During these years, in addition to the perennial problems of help and wages, the owner of the Irvine Ranch had many other troublesome matters, some trivial, some more serious, with which to deal. The members of a boys' Y.M.C.A. camp defaced some of the beautiful oaks in Santiago Cañon, and campers started disastrous fires; the lessee of a prospective oil tract on the ranch had difficulty in fulfilling the terms of his drilling contract, and the hoped-for oil field failed to develop; morning-glory vines became a pest in the bean fields, ticks infested the pastures, and worms damaged the celery; nearly fifty head of cattle and a number of horses died of some unknown disease or diseases; several hunters, including two prominent citizens of Riverside, were arrested for trespassing on pasture lands near Corona del Mar; the Sunset Telephone and Telegraph Company installed a telephone line on company property without the formality of obtaining a right of way; the ranch employees demanded butter with their meals; and a mad dog ran amuck and bit several other dogs on the ranch.

To James Irvine, owner of the ranch, the five years between 1905 and 1910 brought more than his quota of loss and sorrow. When the great earthquake and fire occurred in April 1906, Irvine was not at his home in San Francisco but at the ranch, and he experienced great anxiety over the fate of his wife and children. His office building and other valuable holdings were either destroyed or badly damaged, but he found his wife and children safe upon his return to San Francisco. Irvine and his family then transferred their residence to the ranch, and the three children completed their grammar school education and part of their high school course in Santa Ana.

In 1909, after seventeen years of happy married life, Irvine experienced an irreparable loss in the death of his wife. This tragedy left a deep and abiding hurt in Irvine's life. Something went out of it forever. He became more and more addicted to hunting and fishing and less and less dependent upon the society and companionship of others.

The ranch, however, continued to prosper and to expand both in the magnitude and in the variety of its operations. Experiments with sugar beets proved highly successful, land suitable for the new crop was in great demand, and the ranch opened up numerous tracts to lease for beet farming.

The beets were first sold to the Southern California Sugar Company, which had a factory in Santa Ana, but the arrangement proved unsatisfactory.

"The sugar situation is about the same," Irvine wrote in the fall of 1910. "The factory is handling, if anything, less beets than last year and making all sorts of excuses. Their agitation of big profits &c. has been instrumental in bringing in two new factories, which will be in operation next season. The new factories have contracted more than half of the old factory's acreage. The farmers are all very sore, as many of their beets are still in the ground, and a serious loss faces them, hence they are only too willing to find relief by contracting to other factories. I think they [the company] will have great difficulty in getting sufficient acreage for another year. The management still hang on in their blind contentment."

Soon after this, Irvine organized the Santa Ana Co-operative Sugar Company and built a new factory to provide a more profitable outlet for both the Irvine interests and other sugar-beet producers in the Santa Ana Valley.

To insure its factory an adequate and regular supply, the co-operative company bought some thousands of acres of good sugar-beet land and leased it out to desirable tenants. By 1911, Orange County was producing over 100,000 tons of sugar beets a year. In 1917-18, the Santa Ana company sold its factory to the Holly Sugar Company, and Irvine acquired 350 acres of the old McFadden Ranch on South Main Street in Santa Ana in liquidation of other assets of the company. The Holly Sugar Company still handles all of the sugar beets raised on the Irvine Ranch.

After considerable experiment, Irvine found that the tops of the sugar beets made excellent cattle feed—if the cattle could be taught to eat the new fodder. For the benefit of another rancher he thus outlined the method he finally found most satisfactory:

Prepare corrals, and fence with a 5-wire fence; there should be sufficient troughs attached to a good well of water, with at least two-inch supply pipe, (about one trough 20 feet long for every 50 head of cattle).

Bring over cattle *in the evening* and stand them 24 hours in the corral without feed. Take them out and herd them one hour in the morning and one hour in the evening on the first day.

On the second day herd them two hours morning and evening; and continue the two hour system for three days. Gradually increase the number of hours on the tops from day to day up to the 6th and 7th days, when they should be able to stay all day. Great care should be exercised in the beginning to prevent them overfeeding.

After they have had 6 or 7 days on the tops the close herding should be abandoned, and the cattle should be allowed to drift in and out from the water as they will.

Cows placed on beet tops in fair condition should be ready for beef in 50 or 60 days.

Great care should be taken at all times to see that the cattle do not choke on the beet tops from getting one of the tops in the windpipe. If an animal is seen choking, it should immediately be roped and the instrument applied for holding its mouth open and permitting the hand to reach the beet which is usually found to be stuck about 12 inches (down the throat) from the mouth, the beet should then be extracted. It is possible that there may be some cases where the beet cannot be removed by hand, and then some kind of forceps should be used. It is advisable to use an armlet to keep the cows teeth from injuring the arm.

It may be added in passing that the method of feeding recommended by Irvine was long ago abandoned and that, for the greater safety of man and beast, a piece of rubber hose is now used instead of a man's gauntlet-protected arm to keep an animal from choking to death on beet tops.

In spite of the growth of the sugar-beet industry, beans and barley remained the largest of the field crops, and Irvine took a keen personal interest in their cultivation and harvest, as indeed he then did in all the multitudinous operations of the ranch. In reply to a letter from a farmer in Missouri requesting information on bean culture, the manager of the ranch wrote as follows:

Bean raising requires intense cultivation of the land, somewhat similar to Corn; that is, we plow up the land dry in the Fall, and work it down during the Winter, and plant about the first of May. From that time on we have no rains until after the Beans are in the Warehouse; rarely this rule is broken.

We are now threshing our crop and another month will wind it up. Lima Beans take more or less moisture from the atmosphere and do well along the Coast of Southern California; and all things being equal as regards the quality of the soil, the nearer the Coast the better. On an average the fields are about ten miles from the Ocean. . . .

The average rainfall here is about 10 inches. . . .

A further concise summary of the bean industry on the ranch was sent to the *Chicago Produce News* in October 1911:

We have in Limas about 14,000 acres, and in black-eyes about 4,000 acres, these acreages forming what is stated both here and in Ventura County to be the largest bean field, *under the one management,* in the world. This land is farmed partly by ourselves and in the greater part by tenants who rent on crop shares. The number of sacks raised on this ranch will approximate 145,000 sacks of Limas, and 36,000 blackeyes, or roughly 180,000 sacks of beans which will be worth about $3.50 per sack of 80 lbs when recleaned or say about $630,000.00.

The bean market this year has been exceptionally strong in prices, particularly on Limas, and this in the face of foreign importation of other Limas and "near-lima beans." The yield per acre is not yet so heavy in this section as it is in Ventura County, where the land has been farmed to beans for many years and where the conditions as to fog and other atmospheric influences are supposed to be more favorable than here. We are however improving the yield from year to year, owing to better farming, better selection of seed and the numerous details which lend themselves to successful farming.

Our average crops on the whole ranch are perhaps 10 to 11 sacks per acre, whereas in Ventura County they are not surprised at yields from 25 to 30 sacks per acre, a result which we may some day attain.

The blackeye beans are mainly shipped to the Cotton states and fed to the negroes there. They are not much used here at all, and are known in Missouri and Kansas as blackeye peas. You may know the variety, though we do not think there are many shipped to your section.

No reference to the Lima Bean situation would be complete unless special mention were made of the Lima Bean Growers' Association, which has in three years transformed the business from a disjointed, sell-when-you-can proposition, to a well defined and strong trade, befitting the handling of one of the most important staple articles of food. . . .

State and county taxes on the ranch rose steadily after the turn of the century; and when, in addition to these taxes, Irvine was called upon to pay a corporation tax to the federal government, his indignation found expression in the following vigorous letter:

James Irvine for The Irvine Co. to The Secretary of the Treasury of the United States of America.

To The Commissioner of Internal Revenue of the United States of America.

Gentlemen:

We are herewith forwarding money in payment of our Corporation tax, and also Notice of Protest. We wish to state to you that we consider this one of the most unjust things, in its present form, that this Government has imposed.

If there is any one who does not receive such benefits as may accrue from the formation of trusts, it is the farming community. They are always subject to the hazard of weather and in most cases to all sorts of competition, not at home alone, but from the markets of the world. We are strictly a farming corporation, under a close ownership, being incorporated for various reasons which we felt might at some time be of some advantage to us, but which have not up to the present time.

Of course, we can dis-incorporate if necessary, and thereby avoid this iniquitous tax. Our entire property is represented in land values, and we are already paying a heavy State, County and Bonded tax, which is equivalent to 10 or 15% of our net income. This tax is a constantly increasing one, and yet a greater portion of our land is absolutely dry and our income entirely dependent on the nature of the weather, and dry years in this Western country are not uncommon. It is not unusual in some years not to make a profit, but to incur actual loss.

There are no doubt many forms of Corporations which pay a relatively small tax, and we doubt if there are many that pay the relatively large tax we are paying.

The land is a fixture and cannot escape taxation as you know. We do not know to whom this letter is going but, as Representatives of the Government we wish to express to you our feelings as to the absolute repugnance to this tax, considering it in our case most unjust.

We have always been Republican in our national government affairs, but must say that from now on at least, our sympathies will be strongly with the so-called insurgents.

It may be added that Irvine, despite this irascible outburst, neither disincorporated the Irvine Company nor abandoned the Republican Party, and the ranch soon enjoyed a greater prosperity than it had ever known before.

11

ORCHARDS AND WATER

The development of the citrus industry—today the most profitable of the Irvine Ranch enterprises—began long after most of the other major crops had passed the experimental stage. In 1906, C. E. Utt, a well-known resident of the Santa Ana Valley, conceived a novel plan. At that time, because of the great expense involved, most citrus orchards were only from ten to forty or fifty acres in size.

Utt proposed to his friend Sherman Stevens to lease a thousand acres of rich, adequately watered land and plant the tract to orchards. Utt and Stevens together then interested Irvine in the undertaking, and the three eventually formed a partnership called the San Joaquin Fruit and Investment Company to carry on the work.

Under the agreement, Irvine entered the partnership on the same terms as the other two; the Irvine Company agreed to lease a thousand acres of selected land on the Rancho San Joaquin to the partnership for a term of ten years; after four years, the partners had the right to buy all the land that had been set out to orchard at two hundred dollars an acre; the lessees obligated themselves to bear the entire expense of planting and caring for the orchards; water for irrigation was to be developed in the swampy lowlands of the ranch and lifted to the orchards, at the lessees' expense; and the Irvine Company, on its part, agreed to sell ten acres of such water-bearing land to the partnership for a thousand dollars.

Under this contract, the San Joaquin Fruit and Investment Company planted six hundred acres to walnuts and apricots and four hundred acres to oranges and lemons. Before the orchards came into commercial bearing, the lessees planted lima beans, peanuts, chili peppers, and nursery stock between the tree rows to help defray the heavy costs of the undertaking. At the end of the ten-year period, the Irvine Company deeded the thousand acres to the three partners in accordance with the terms of the lease, and the partners eventually sold some six hundred acres of mature, heavily bearing trees at approximately thirty-five hundred dollars an acre.

Long before this, the success of the San Joaquin Fruit Company's venture led the Irvine Company itself to plant many hundreds of additional acres to oranges and lemons.

All this land, of course, required irrigation, and fortunately at that time there was ample water on the ranch to meet the additional demands. But serious lack of rainfall during the autumn and early winter of 1911-12, the driest comparable period in thirty-five years, reduced the beet and bean crops by nearly half and forced the ranch to look for new pasturage for its cattle in the Palo Verde Valley along the route of the Santa Fe railroad to Phoenix, Arizona.

The drought was followed by the Great Freeze of January 1913. This proved a major disaster to many of the citrus growers of southern California, but the comparatively young groves of the Irvine Ranch suffered much less than many of the surrounding orchards. Irvine was at the ranch when the freeze struck and on January 8 wrote to his manager in San Francisco:

It has been extremely cold here, near and below freezing point almostly constantly for three days. On Monday night the temperature in the young lemon orchard was 22, and last night from 24 to 32 for over nine hours. The most serious damage ever done has undoubtedly occurred, generally throughout the citrus districts. Smudging has helped some on the various orchards, but the temperatures are almost too low to handle, unless an unusual number of pots are used. Those not smudging lost heavily, in many cases probably the entire crop. The [San Joaquin] Fruit Co. I think is hurt some, but we cannot tell yet. Browning claims to be only partially hurt, but he smudged very heavily.[1] Our own lemons and those of the Krauss orchard are not bearing, but from examination today it looks as if the trees were not killed. We burned several hundred bales of bean straw among the lemons.

Two days later, Irvine wrote again:

It is impossible to tell how much damage has been done, but it is more than ever exemplified that the ranch is the least frosty district in probably the whole citrus belt. Some of the orange crops in Tustin are practically ruined. Browning through very heavy smudging probably kept his loss down to 10 or 15 per cent. The Fruit Co. estimate the loss on their fruit at probably 10 to 15 per cent, confined mostly to the very small lemons which would have made the high priced lemons next summer. It will take some time to determine the full loss. While unquestionably heavy in places I believe the loss has been less than one might expect from the extreme low sustained temperatures, which ranged from 22° to a few degrees above the freezing point for 48 hours or more.

The ten or fifteen per cent loss of its citrus crop by the San Joaquin Fruit Company was much more than counterbalanced by the abnormally high prices the good fruit com-

[1]F. B. Browning was a former manager of the Irvine Ranch.

manded, and fortunately the trees suffered no permanent damage from the unprecedented cold.

Despite the freeze of 1913, the Irvine Company greatly expanded its planting of citrus and other fruit trees during the next twenty years and made a corresponding reduction in field crop acreage. Low-lying areas were drained; considerable land previously devoted to cattle and sheep pasture was brought under cultivation; after 1917 several hundred acres each year were planted to tomatoes and additional large areas to lettuce, cabbage, mustard, peas, rhubarb, and other vegetables; and millions of dollars were spent on water conservation and development.

In 1921, the San Joaquin Fruit and Investment Company negotiated a second lease with the Irvine Company that differed in some important details but followed in general the pattern set by the original lease of 1906. The new lease included only two hundred and forty acres; it ran for fifteen years; at the end of that period, the San Joaquin Fruit and Investment Company agreed to pay a thousand dollars an acre for the land, and during the life of the lease the Irvine Company was to receive a twenty-five per cent interest in the share-rental of the property. The lessees planted some two hundred acres of the new tract to avocados and the rest to oranges.

In 1930, the Utt Development Company, half of whose stock was owned by the San Joaquin Fruit and Investment Company, bought a section of land near Oxnard in Ventura County and undertook the development of a large lemon orchard. An additional hundred and sixty acres were added to the tract in 1940. In spite of a number of unforeseen problems, the venture proved an excellent investment. Part of the success of the enterprise was due to the management's careful study of root stocks, desirable buds, and proper methods of pruning. The company also used wind machines in combating damage by frost with good results. In 1950 some forty machines were in operation on the Oxnard ranch.

In the mid-twenties the San Joaquin Fruit Company bought another large tract, called Walnut Acres, in the San Fernando Valley, but when it was proposed to subdivide and sell the land, Irvine became skeptical of the outcome of the venture and exchanged his interests in the property for three hundred acres, valued at approximately half a million dollars, that the San Joaquin Fruit Company still held in the Irvine Ranch.

Many purchasers of land in Walnut Acres defaulted on their contracts as a result of the panic of 1929, and Utt and Stevens found their San Fernando property a heavy financial liability. Irvine then took over part of Utt's stock to lighten the latter's load.

At the present time the San Joaquin Fruit and Investment Company owns two hundred and ten acres of the Irvine Ranch and still holds its half interest in the Utt Development Company. The latter has liquidated its holdings in the San Fernando Valley, however, as well as certain properties it formerly owned near Seal Beach.

As the Irvine Ranch came more and more under diversified and intensive cultivation, the problem of obtaining an adequate supply of water became increasingly difficult and insistent. The full-scale development of the company's water resources included the most economical use of that part of the flow of Santiago Creek to which the ranch was entitled, the sinking or drilling of many hundreds of wells in the Santa Ana basin, the construction of storage reservoirs

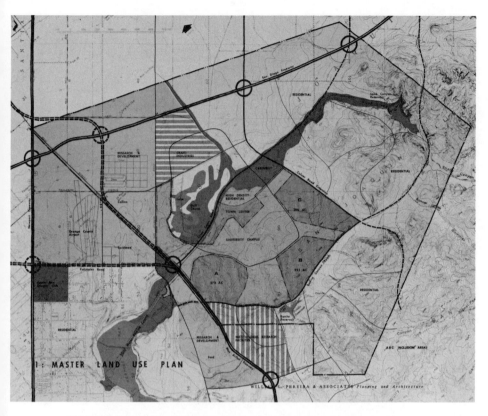

MASTER PLAN FOR THE UNIVERSITY OF CALIFORNIA AT IRVINE
AND THE SURROUNDING AREA

ARCHITECT'S DRAWING OF PROJECTED NEWPORT CENTER
*Complex of buildings to be built near Newport Bay (on Coast
Highway between Jamboree and MacArthur boulevards) symbolizes
the kind of planning now under way at the Irvine Company*

and flood control dams in all feasible places, and, finally, the effective and economical distribution of the water developed or conserved by these various means.

Much of the low-lying land on the Irvine Ranch was originally overgrown with willows, tules, and water grasses and was so wet and marshy as to require extensive drainage by means of ditches and tile lines. Water for irrigation came from shallow wells, some of which were artesian in character; but as more and more of the land was drained and a much larger acreage placed under irrigation, the demand upon the underground supply, the accumulation of untold ages, was more than the normal rainfall could replace, and in times of long-continued drought, the heavy withdrawal from these natural subsurface reservoirs offered a serious threat to the ranch's future water reserves.

As early as 1910, Irvine believed the ranch could profitably use an additional thousand inches of water from outside sources; but since this was not available he added more and more wells until he had drilled some twelve hundred altogether and spent between three and four million dollars in the process.

The expansion of irrigation and the dry years of the twenties led the Irvine Company to introduce a major program of water conservation and incidental flood control by means of dams and storage reservoirs on the various streams belonging to the ranch. The list of such additions included the Lambert Reservoir (1929), the Santiago Cañon Dam (1931-32), the Peters Cañon Dam No. 1, Laguna Dam, Bonita Dam (1937-38), the Peters Cañon Dam No. 2 (1940), the Sand Cañon Dam (1942), and the Syphon Cañon Dam (1948-49). The total storage capacity of these various dams and reservoirs is close to 30,000 acre feet.

The dam across Santiago Cañon that forms Irvine Lake is by far the largest of the foregoing undertakings. The dam is of the earth-filled type, contains approximately 1,110,000 cubic yards of material, has a concrete face as protection against wave action, and has a concrete spillway. The Irvine Company furnished the site for the reservoir and bore half the cost of constructing the dam. The remaining funds were supplied by the Serrano and Carpenter irrigation districts on equal shares.[2]

The dam conserves the water of a sixty-five-square-mile drainage area in the Santa Ana Mountains and at spillway level is capable of storing 25,000 acre feet of water. Its completion "marked the harmonious conclusion of much argument and litigation" that arose from conflicting claims over rights to runoff waters. Roughly speaking, the Irvine Company is entitled to fifty per cent of the water in storage; but its withdrawal of the water is restricted by a number of factors, including that of rainfall.

Even with Irvine Lake and the other water conservation reservoirs, the Irvine Ranch found itself faced with an ever-growing water shortage as a result of the abnormally low rainfall that plagued southern California, including the Santa Ana Valley, after 1943. The water situation was rendered much more critical by the large overexpansion of agriculture, the huge influx of population, and the rapid industrial growth of southern California during the booming forties. Only Los Angeles, with its life-saving Owens River Aqueduct, and those other cities and communities that belonged to the Metropolitan Water District of Southern Cali-

[2]Half of the water of Santiago Creek is owned by the Irvine Company and half by the Serrano and Carpenter irrigation districts. The Irvine Company and the two water districts lease the fishing rights on Irvine Lake to a company that caters to the public.

fornia and thereby had access to the flow of the Colorado River enjoyed immunity from this widely prevalent and increasingly dangerous water shortage.

As the years went by and the cycle of abnormally low rainfall continued, both urban and agricultural districts in the Santa Ana Valley began to look to the Metropolitan Water District as their only hope of relief and ultimate salvation. A plan was devised to combine a number of cities and some 200,000 acres of agricultural and potential residential lands, having an assessed valuation of about two hundred million dollars, into a single district to obtain Colorado River water from the Metropolitan Water District to supplement the local supply of Orange County.

Under the proposed plan, some of the water would be treated for use by the urban communities in the new district, while untreated water for irrigation would be delivered to the Santa Ana Valley and Anaheim Irrigation District canals in Santa Ana Cañon and to Santiago Reservoir (Irvine Lake) for the Serrano and Carpenter irrigation districts and the Irvine Ranch.

Engineers estimated that such a plan would cost in the neighborhood of $13,000,000, and the Metropolitan District expected to charge ten dollars an acre foot, in addition to taxes, for water supplied for irrigation. But it is an old saying in southern California that water at almost any price is cheap, and from the standpoint of the Santa Ana Valley as a whole and the Irvine Ranch in particular, the plan, which promised to stabilize the heretofore dangerously fluctuating water supply and eliminate the recurrent threat of drought, had the unanswerable argument of necessity to commend it.

Like many other large owners, James Irvine was a strong

supporter of the co-operative principle of marketing farm products. The Irvine Ranch joined the California Fruit Growers Exchange (now Sunkist Growers, Inc.)—the largest and one of the oldest organizations of its kind in the world—at a very early date and sells its oranges through three branches of the exchange—the Irvine Valencia Growers Association, the Golden West Citrus Association, and the Frances Citrus Association.

The company's lemons are handled by the Irvine Citrus Association; its walnuts by the California Walnut Growers Association; its lima beans by the California Lima Bean Growers Association; its persimmons by the California Persimmon Growers Association; and its avocados by Calavo Growers of California. The ranch sells its cattle on an independent basis but otherwise relies on the co-operative associations for which California has long been noted.

In addition to its agricultural assets, at least in earlier years, the Irvine Ranch also had a number of small gypsum deposits and enough coal in the mountains of the Lomas de Santiago Ranch to warrant small-scale development. In 1908 the Orange County Coal Mining Company, with offices in the Mason Building at Fourth and Broadway, Los Angeles, operated a mine in Santiago Cañon which it described at some length in an illustrated and not altogether unalluring prospectus. The description began:

Coal in Southern California

That there is coal, good coal, in Southern California will be a surprise to many, but this is an established fact.

There is one operated Coal Mining property in Southern California and WE OWN IT.

This property is located in Santiago Canyon, Orange County, California, about 35 miles from Los Angeles, 14 miles from Santa

Ana, 10 miles from Orange and less than 7 miles by a good road from McPherson Station on the Southern Pacific railroad.

The extent of our coal lands, the richness of the coal deposits, and the superior qualities of the coal itself, have all been thoroughly determined by some of the best coal experts in the country.

This property has been worked in a primitive way for the past twelve years, and over 20,000 tons of surface coal mined and sold, furnishing fuel for mills and private consumers in Santa Ana, Orange, Anaheim and surrounding country.

The brochure also assured prospective investors in the company of large profits and "quick returns," but the promise somehow failed to reach fulfillment.

By 1900, the oil industry had become one of southern California's major enterprises, and Irvine bought stock in at least six local companies.[3] One of these, the Senator Oil Company, undertook to build a pipeline across the ranch, and Irvine eventually agreed to accept the company's bonds in payment for a right of way. The company afterward merged with the Associated Oil Company.

Irvine at this time also made a large number of oil leases on the ranch. Such a lease usually covered a full section or 640 acres, ran for twenty years, reserved an eighth royalty to the landowner, called for a cash payment of a hundred dollars when the lease was signed, and required drilling to start within four months.

None of these early leases led to the production of oil in commercial quantities, nor have subsequent attempts proved much more successful. In 1949, some 50,000 acres of the ranch were included in an exploration agreement with the Shell Oil Company, and after extensive geological

[3]These included the West Shore Oil Company, Puente Crude Oil Company, Central Point Oil Company, Section Four Oil Company, Aztec Oil Company, and Senator Oil Company.

and geophysical exploration, the company drilled three wells at widely distant points, but no significant discoveries were made.

In 1934, the Irvine Company built a plant to produce salt by solar evaporation on the northern end of Upper Newport Bay. Extensive evaporating ponds and crystallizing vats occupy some 250 acres, and annual production in 1950 ran about 6,000 tons. The great floods of 1937-38 caused extensive damage to the works and carried most of the year's "crop" out to sea. The salt is sold only for industrial uses.

It is not generally known, at least beyond the bounds of Orange County, that the Irvine Ranch was the scene of one of the most important pioneer airplane developments in the United States. In 1909, Glenn L. Martin, then at the beginning of his distinguished career as aviator, engineer, and airplane manufacturer, built a crude plane in an abandoned church in Santa Ana and made his first flight from a portion of the Irvine Ranch now bounded by Newport and Lane roads in the immediate vicinity of the present Orange County Airport.

In addition to giving him permission to use the necessary land for his runway, James Irvine took a keen personal interest in Martin's venture and even accompanied the young aviator on an experimental flight during which the plane reached a height of over seven hundred feet, attained a speed of fifty-five miles an hour, and remained in the air for twenty minutes. On May 10, 1912, Martin flew the same plane from Newport to Catalina Island. The following description of the flight appeared in the Santa Ana *Register* of May 11.

Glenn L. Martin of Santa Ana yesterday became world famous. He flew his hydro-aeroplane from Newport Bay to Avalon, a distance of 34 miles, and back again. The flight across was made in 37 minutes, while the return flight took him 51 minutes. In making his flight, he accomplished the greatest cross-water flight ever made by man.

On Martin's knee was strapped a compass, by which he set his course. On his wrist was a watch by which he judged the distance traveled, for he figured on going nearly a mile a minute. Before him was an aneroid barometer, by which he knew approximately the distance above the earth.

Many years after his early association with Martin's pioneer ventures in the field of aviation, Irvine again showed his deep interest in scientific research by allowing Albert A. Michelson, one of the outstanding physicists of the past generation, to use a mile-long strip of ranch land for his famous experiment in the measurement of the velocity of light.

12

URBAN PRESSURES

In addition to the developments previously noted, the past four or five decades have witnessed many significant events in the history of the Irvine Ranch. One of these involved a concerted effort on the part of a group of attorneys and an organization called the Homesteaders Association to invalidate the United States patents to many of the old Spanish-Mexican California land grants, return the land to the public domain, and throw it open again to pre-emption. The Lomas de Santiago was a special target for the efforts of this group, a number of whom were subsequently indicted for using the United States mails with intent to defraud. Before this action was taken by the Department of Justice, however, the movement had become so widespread and showed itself possessed of such incalculable elements of mischief that the United States Senate instructed its Committee on Public Lands and Surveys to make a thorough investigation of its activities and render a report to the Senate. The report was entitled *Mexican Land Grant Frauds* and published by order of the Senate of the 69th Congress, second session, at the Government Printing Office, Washington, D.C., in 1927.

The methods and procedure of the instigators of the land-grant attacks were described as follows in the committee's findings:

Charges had been made and repeated with frequency that vast areas of land in southern California were held under fraudulent titles arising from the fact that in some instances no grant was ever made by the Government of Spain or that of Mexico; in some instances forged or fabricated grants had been obtained; in some cases grants, although issued subsequent to the treaty of Guadalupe Hidalgo, had been antedated to precede American sovereignty, and in other instances a grant was made of a fixed quantity of land, but that in surveying and fixing the boundaries of such grant, a vast quantity in excess of the original grant was included in the field notes and the patent subsequently issued, thus passing into private possession such excess land which, in fact, is the property of the United States and constitutes a part of the public domain, and, accordingly, is properly subject to homestead entry. A so-called Homesteaders Association was formed with offices in Los Angeles, Calif. The practice of those in charge of such association was to solicit persons eligible to make homestead entry on the public domain to file on these lands, the association charging a filing fee plus a legal retainer fee for such services, varying from $100 to $1,000.

This practice has extended over a period of several years and has netted officers and agents of the association a stupendous financial reward. According to information furnished the committee, it is still followed in some form. It was the common practice of the officers or agents of the association to take prospective applicants out and show them lands with the statement and representation that they were available for entry. In most instances these lands were highly improved, with bearing orchards, vineyards, productive farms, and modern dwellings thereon. In some instances they included towns of substantial size with brick buildings and other expensive improvements of incalculable value. These applicants were told that through appropriate action of Congress or the courts, title of the present occupants and their predecessors in interest would be held invalid; that thereupon such lands would be subject to homestead entry and that the applications of these persons would take priority, thus vesting them with title and possession of some of the most highly improved and valuable farms and suburban property in southern California, some of which is adjacent to the city of Los Angeles. As stated, the Homesteaders Association in virtually every case charged a filing fee plus a legal retainer fee, usually being from $100 to $1,000, for the alleged service thus rendered and to be rendered in pressing the rights of the applicant either before the Department of the Interior or Congress or in the courts. Pursuant to this system many scores of applications were filed covering large quantities of land.

At least two hundred "homesteaders," claiming that the United States still had legal title to at least seven of the eleven square leagues included in the grant, prepared to file on the lands of the Rancho Lomas de Santiago. Attempts were made to have both the Department of the Interior and the President revoke the patent and to test the validity of title in the courts. The ramifications of the case in Washington were both extensive and prolonged, but when the Secretary of the Interior sought the opinion of the Attorney General, the answer was conclusive:

Dear Mr. Secretary: Your letter of December 4, 1924, referred to this department the question of the advisability of a suit by the Government to reform the patent of February 1, 1868, to the Rancho Lomas de Santiago in Orange County, Calif., transmitting briefs relating thereto filed by counsel in the matter affecting this property, which had been pending in the Interior Department.

The questions presented by this reference have been exhaustively considered, extensive hearings have been held, and all parties interested have been heard at length, and voluminous documents have been examined in reaching a conclusion. Without going into details I deem it sufficient to advise you that no suit should be instituted for the following reasons:

First. Any action attempted to be maintained would be barred by the statute of limitations of March 3, 1891, 26 Stat. 1093.

Second. The issues involved in such litigation are res adjudicata by the cases of United States *v.* Yorba (1856-1858); United States *v.* Flint (1875-1878) 4 Sawyer, 42.

Third. The institution of such a suit would be a third attack by the Government upon the title to this land. Sound public policy does not require that new litigation shall be instituted to disturb the rule of property established in California by United States *v.* Flint, where no new facts are submitted and no showing made that former executive officials were clearly wrong in their action in reference to these cases.

Fourth. The two suits mentioned were dismissed on appeal to the Supreme Court by former Attorneys General, with the same subject matter and the same relief involved. The transcript in the Supreme Court in the case of United States *v.* Flint (1878), clearly shows that the decision of that court can not be successfully avoided. Prior to the dismissal of this case, upon motion of the Solicitor General, the Supreme Court had said:

"So far as we can discover from the records, the only matter in dispute is the ownership of the land in controversy, the United States claiming it on the one hand and the appellees on the other."

Respectfully,

Jno. G. Sargent, *Attorney General.*

The opinion of the Attorney General left little shadow on the title to the Rancho Lomas de Santiago, and the report of the Committee on Public Lands to the United States Senate presumably ended once and for all such wholesale attacks on California land-grant titles as those instigated by the organizers of the Homesteaders Association of the midtwenties. A concluding section of the report ran as follows:

It is the judgment of the committee that the grants in question are separately and severally valid; that their confirmation in conformity with the provisions of the act of March 3, 1851, constitute res adjudicata and can not be reviewed; that no fraud in connection with its issuance being shown, the patent in each case is conclusively binding with respect to the quantity of land conveyed; that such confirmation of title and issuance of patent present a perfect case of repose of title and foreclose further question; that the attacks being made upon such titles are without substance or foundation and are inspired and furthered by persons seeking to profit financially at the expense of well intentioned but grossly misled applicants for homestead entry.

Your committee is unanimously of the opinion that those now claiming the lands in question, as successors in interest under the original grants, confirmed as hereinbefore stated, are the unqalified owners thereof and have an unquestioned legal title thereto, and that there is no foundation in fact or in law for the charges which Senate Resolution 291 directed this committee to investigate.

Following the outbreak of World War II, the United States government requisitioned 2,318 acres in the center of the Irvine Ranch, near the town of Irvine, and there established the Marine Corps Air Station, El Toro. The base was extremely active during the war and is still the largest station of its kind in California, now totaling 3,722 acres.[1]

On another tract of 1,600 acres, near the city of Tustin, the government also established a lighter-than-air station for dirigibles and built two huge hangars, each approximately a thousand feet long. The station has been converted into a helicopter training center.

One of the greatest assets of the Irvine Company, especially today, is its long ocean frontage. The ranch runs almost continuously along the coast from Newport Bay to Laguna, a distance of eight miles. Most of this long stretch is as yet unsubdivided or undeveloped, largely because of difficult sewage disposal problems, but the amazing increase of population, especially in the Los Angeles metropolitan area, the climatic conditions in southern California,

[1]Because of the name, the air base is often confused with the community of El Toro which lies several miles farther south.

and the ever-increasing demand for vacation and recreation facilities give to the Irvine ocean-front properties a value, both present and potential, of which an older generation never dreamed.

As owners of much of the mainland and some of the islands in Newport Bay, the Irvine Company has attempted to follow a constructive policy, for both the immediate and the distant future, in the development of its properties. When the Newport harbor was improved in the mid-thirties, Irvine joined with the city and other property owners in an exchange of land for straightening and widening the channels. He also bought dredgings from the harbor operations and provided areas for their disposition.[2]

The Irvine Company has subdivided a number of tracts near Newport Bay. One of these, the Bayshores Tract, is situated between two channels of the bay on the ocean side of the Coast Highway, officially known as "Alternate 101," for which the Irvine Company gave without cost the long and valuable right of way.[3] The Balboa Bay Club occupies a large area, owned by the city of Newport Beach, directly to the west. The Irvine subdivision known as Cliff Haven is situated on the landward side of Bayshores Tract, upon the mesa, and fronts on the palisades. In its subdivisions, the company has usually followed the practice

[2]The great increase of population and the shortage of water as a result of the decrease of the flow in the Santa Ana River basin led the city of Newport Beach to join the Metropolitan Water District of Southern California in 1942.

In the early 1900's, as previously noted, the Irvine Company sold a tract of land to George E. Hart upon which the city of Corona del Mar has since been built. The Irvine Beach and Country Club Estates, a subdivision undertaken during the depression, made little headway at that time but has subsequently become a part of the city of Newport Beach and is now known as Shore Cliffs and Corona Highlands.

[3]The company also donated valuable water rights to the city of Newport.

of offering long-term leases instead of making outright sales.

The Irvine Company also has extensive interests in the city of Laguna Beach at the extreme southern limit of the Irvine Ranch. The city was originally a small, isolated beach community, reached only by a rough wagon road through Laguna Cañon, a portion of which marks the boundary line between the Irvine Ranch and Rancho Niguel.

The community's water supply was then so brackish and inadequate that householders for many years hauled water for domestic use from a small stream in upper Laguna Cañon that was fed by the Laguna Lakes. Later the water was piped to one section of the town.

That part of the Irvine Ranch included in Laguna Beach is commonly known as the Laguna Cliffs and lies for the most part northwest of the bed of Laguna Cañon. Part of this property was sold to various persons, including Otis Jones and H. G. Heisler, and another section now known as Emerald Bay was bought originally by the Miles and Callender interests.

The construction of the coastal highway in the mid-twenties for which the Irvine Company, as already mentioned, gave the right of way through the ranch, stimulated the growth of numerous beach communities south of Newport Bay. The rapid growth of population created a severe water problem for Laguna Beach. Irvine agreed to finance and build a large pipeline to bring water from the Santa Ana River basin to the city, and upon completion of the line he sold approximately a half interest in the enterprise to the Laguna Beach County Water District. In 1933, a suit was brought to enjoin this diversion of water from the Santa Ana watershed, but the Irvine Company and Laguna Beach successfully resisted the suit and won the right to take a specified quantity of water from the basin. All rights of way for the pipeline were donated by the company, and the latter's maintenance of easement rights over the state highway also saved Laguna Beach the heavy costs incident to relaying the line when the State Highway Commission subsequently made numerous changes in the grades and location of the highway.

Even with the large pipeline, the depletion of the water supply in the Santa Ana basin threatened to affect Laguna Beach even more seriously than most other cities that drew their water from the same source. As a result, the Coastal Municipal Water District was created to enable the area to join the Metropolitan Water District of Southern California. At the present time, nearly all of the water used in the community is supplied by the flow of the Colorado River, but certain emergency, stand-by connections are still maintained in the Santa Ana River basin.

The continued interest of the Irvine family in Laguna Beach was shown some years ago by the company's donation of the "Irvine Bowl," and some adjoining acreage, to provide the city with necessary recreational and cultural facilities. The Bowl soon became an indispensable community institution and made possible the present development of the famous Laguna Art Festival.

On August 24, 1947, two men, who often fished and hunted together, were working a stream that ran through the Irvine Company's recently acquired Flying D Ranch, near Bozeman, Montana.

One of the two was William Bradford Hellis, who had been in the employ of the Irvine Ranch since as early as 1914. In 1923 he had been made secretary of the company and ten years later had become its general manager (which he remained until his retirement in May 1959) with extensive control over all the activities of the ranch. To its owner, he was friend, companion, and adviser.

The other fisherman on Spanish Creek that August day was James Irvine, owner of the Irvine Ranch, son of its founder, and for well over half a century the director of its policies and operations.

The two men were fishing apart—Hellis upstream, Irvine below. One wonders what thoughts and memories ran through Irvine's mind that day. Perhaps he was intent only on his fishing, for he was passionately devoted to the sport. Perhaps he recalled his boyhood visits to the Irvine Ranch when Los Angeles was still half Mexican pueblo, Santa Ana scarcely a crossroads town, and the ranch no more than "a sheep walk, waste and wide." Perhaps he reviewed the transformation of the ranch during the long years of his ownership and saw in retrospect the thousands upon thousands of acres of once uninhabited pasture lands give way to rich, cultivated fields, heavily productive orchards, well-ordered farms, profitable alike to himself and to the tenant; perhaps —with the rivers and streams of the Flying D to revive his memory—he reviewed his never-ceasing efforts to increase and conserve the vital water supply of his thirsty southern lands; perhaps he thought of the fortune that the subdivision of his miles of ocean frontage would some day bring, or even of the time when the flood tide of population, engulfing all of southern California, would force a breakup of the great ranch itself.

But whatever Irvine's thoughts and memories that day on Spanish Creek, they had no opportunity to run their normal course. A Companion, of whose presence the fisherman was unaware, walked beside him along the stream, watched him make his final cast, and quietly spoke his name. The summons was one that none of the sons of man has ever disobeyed.

Coming downstream, Hellis found the lifeless body of James Irvine partly submerged in the pleasant waters of Spanish Creek.

When James Irvine died in the solitude of his Montana ranch, he left as direct descendants a son, Myford, three granddaughters, and two great-grandchildren.[4]

His elder son, James Irvine, III (usually called Jase), had died tragically of tuberculosis in 1935, and hence never came to the presidency. He had, however, served the company as vice-president for many years in the late twenties and early thirties. After 1932 his father often wished he could give the whole ranch in exchange for his elder son's health. Jase was a hard-working Irvine, and his wife used to tease him that he loved the ranch more than he did her.

The second son, Myford, then forty-nine, succeeded his father as president of the Irvine Company in 1947. A resident of the San Francisco Bay region and graduate of Stanford University, he had made a place for himself in the business life of San Francisco and played an especially important part in the activities of the Society of California

---

[4]Kathryn Helena in 1920 and James in 1935 both predeceased their father. The three grandchildren were Kathryn Anita Lillard (Mrs. Charles S. Wheeler, III), Kathryn Helena Irvine's daughter; Athalie Anita (Mrs. Richard Burt), known as Joan, daughter of the elder son, James Irvine, III; and Myford's daughter, Linda Jane (Mrs. M. Keith Gaede). (Myford Irvine's second child, James Myford Irvine, was born in 1953.) In 1931, James Irvine, II, had married Kathryn Brown White; there were no children of this marriage.

Pioneers, an organization that his grandfather had helped to establish and of which he himself had served as president.

Although his official home was in northern California, Myford Irvine had spent much of his boyhood and later years on the Irvine Ranch. Possessing a good working knowledge of its operations, he foresaw its ever-expanding possibilities. In 1949 he moved to San Marino and the next year took up his residence in the sedate ranch house where the Irvine family had lived since 1900.

Myford Irvine's grandfather had created the ranch and carried it through the pioneer or pastoral stage of its development. His father had developed it into one of the largest, most productive fruit, grain, and bean ranches in the state. Myford's own unique opportunity and responsibility lay in the development of a large section of the ranch not for cattle, sheep, orchards, or field crops, but for the use and enjoyment of people.

EPILOGUE

BY ROBERT V. HINE

On April 22, 1961, like their predecessors for four generations, the range hands of the Irvine Ranch gathered in Bommer Canyon for the spring roundup. The white-faced cattle were corralled and separated. Above the canyon, cloud shadows felt out the contours of the soft hills; hawks circled lazily, alert for the stench of burning hair and hide; and the JI brand seared flesh just as it had for the first bearer of its initials. The scene was timeless; the job was immemorial. More than a thousand calves had been dropped that year. Buyers watched. Cows bawled after missing offspring.

Much was old, but much was also new. No longer were the irons heated in a wood fire, but by butane. Station wagons had brought over the neighboring ranchers, the *rancheros visitadores*, and prosperity was in their every smile, in their suede jackets and neatly pressed slacks ranged atop the corral fence. And beside these new trappings lay an unexpressed but clear feeling that the whole spectacle —ropings and prizes and ensuing barbecue included—could not persist too much longer. It was of the past, and the Irvine Ranch since 1946 had embarked on a new era, a phase which would be compounded of electronics plants, pedestrian malls, green belts, high-rises, yacht basins, and college campuses. The spring roundup would not cease; cattle would roam Irvine hills for many more decades; but they would become a less and less significant part of the total complex of company activities.

In the second half of the twentieth century, however, against the impression of imminent change, the ranch remains above all a tradition. Of course, a tradition, too, is a changing thing, living, reshaping itself, always partly dying and partly being reborn, yet moving within predetermined guidelines. Perhaps it is these traces which are being jumped; here may be the mark of change.

Certainly it is true that the predominant tradition of the ranch—the massive lines which have remained strong in spite of occasional breaks or bulges—has been agricultural. The basic patterns—the balance between tenancy, joint operations, and the company's own direct farming; the diversification between orchard and field; the continued reliance on co-operative marketing of many field crops and all tree crops—these alter little through the years. Of the forty-eight agricultural tenants on the ranch, thirty-two have been leasing for ten years or longer; four, over twenty-five years; and three additional leases have gone into the second generation. The number of acres in grains (barley, oats, wheat), beans, alfalfa, sugar beets, chili peppers, and tomatoes has in recent times remained fairly constant, except for certain increases near the foothills made possible by new reservoirs and a general increase in vegetable farming.[1]

In orchards, covering 5,500 acres, the last decade has seen a dramatic expansion of citrus. Between 1950 and 1961 under pressure of increasing land values, Valencia orange acreage in the state decreased roughly forty per cent, and in Orange County the drop in that period was fifty per cent, from 60,833 acres to 30,400 acres. A traditional agricultural operation might logically take advantage of the economic situation and increase its production whenever a future demand can be easily predicted. Between 1958 and 1964 about 1,500 acres of new Irvine citrus are planned, and in 1961 one half of this program is already completed.

The citrus expansion is chiefly in Valencia oranges. For these the ranch's fertile valleys behind coastal hills have proved to be a prime producing area—a soft Mediterranean zone, warm enough to encourage sweetness, close enough to the coast to avoid excessive frost.

[1]Irvine Ranch agriculture, 1950 and 1960 (in acres)

Tree Crops	1950 ranch proper	1950 joint orchards	1960 ranch proper	1960 joint orchards
oranges	3,052	837	3,238	896
lemons	522	155	471	145
grapefruit	104	13	104	28
walnuts	690	31	559	0
persimmons	57	0	69	0
avocados	70	0	60	0

Field Crops	ranch proper	tenants	ranch proper	tenants
grains	2,736	4,790	4,222	3,375
black-eyed beans	0	3,918	0	1,747
lima beans	0	5,735	0	5,693
alfalfa	77	882	0	937
sugar beets	0	631	0	372
chili peppers	0	0	0	377
tomatoes	0	40	0	171
misc. (incl. flower seeds; other veg.)	0	588	0	1,816

For the majestic walnut tree, on the other hand, the same area is proving to be less and less desirable. Drought years have dried up the deep moisture; mild winters have hindered dormancy; and northern California has gradually usurped the field. The Irvine Ranch, the last major walnut grower in southern California, will during the next five years slowly phase out its walnut groves. The standing patriarchs, spreading their deep-shade canopy, some of them seventy-five years old, will fall, and in their place will go Valencia oranges.

The new Valencias will not be the same as their predecessors. Like primitive peoples succumbing to unaccustomed diseases, orange orchards of the area have been swept with a plague called "quick decline" (Tristeza), and dying trees with brown leaves or bare branches stand as lonely pariahs in most groves. The company expects the disease to claim one half of the 325,000 orange trees now on the ranch. It is a major catastrophe, and up to now nothing can be done except remove the dead and replant with resistant root stock.[2] At the same time, the new trees are being set out much closer to one another. Where fifty years ago plantings averaged fifty per acre, they now tend nearer one hundred. The eventual yield, though smaller per tree, is substantially larger per acre.

Thus a complicated transitional process goes on, and, like a military operation in modern warfare, it moves on many fronts. As walnuts are phased out and as "quick decline" claims its toll, new orange stock is planted and in more intensive patterns.

Regarding livestock, the number of head of cattle has not

[2]Sweet orange, Troyer citrange, or Cleopatra mandarin, instead of the sour-root stocks.

changed materially in the last ten years. The breeding herd stands more or less steady at 1,200 cows and 85 bulls. With the calf crop averaging ninety-three per cent, the total herd approaches 4,000, more or less, depending on the time of year. The series of dry winters culminating in 1960-61, however, left the range so deficient in grass that in the spring of 1961 the she-stock had been pruned to about 700 cows; but given greener hillsides the herd will be gradually restored to its normal strength.

Cattle still roam the ranch's thousand hills, but the sound of bleating sheep has gone, probably forever. From the 1860's when the first James Irvine could count a crop of 40,000 lambs alone, the Irvines for nearly a century had continuously clipped wool. But by the 1950's sheep raising had become increasingly difficult and decreasingly profitable. Not only did synthetic fabrics wrench the wool market, but the problem of constantly moving the animals, a necessary part of sheep raising, became a major hurdle as freeways began to throw concrete and wire barriers across the ranges. On June 27, 1958, the company's president reported to the directors that the Irvine Ranch no longer had any investment in sheep.

No problem overshadows ranch minds more than the supply of water; the reduction of the cattle herd would so attest, if any proof were needed. As in the old song, the devil who spreads the burning land with mirage must be captured and made to produce. The company now has some eighty wells pumping from the underground basin; it has riparian rights from its two miles of property bordering the Santa Ana River; but in years of calamitous drought and expanding populations, the local sources are beginning to seem driblets. In the early 1950's wells were deepened and more efficient pumps installed; and yet even the underground basin had limits.

So it is easy to understand why the first pouring of the Colorado River water via the Santiago Lateral Pipeline into Irvine reservoirs was for the ranch perhaps the most important single event of the decade. Following long negotiations conducted for the company by its general manager, W. B. Hellis, the conveyance of right of way to the Metropolitan Water District was completed in 1955, and in December of 1956 the first Colorado River water flowed into the Irvine's Santiago Reservoir. On July 1, 1957, the cost for untreated water to the company was $12.00 per acre foot, with one tenth of the water lost in evaporation. Following its availability the ranch has purchased annually between three thousand and twenty thousand acre feet of Colorado River water, representing in recent years up to sixty-five per cent of the total water used.

At the same time, the reservoir system itself has been expanded by the construction of the Rattlesnake Canyon Dam. Plans were approved in May 1959, construction was completed within seven months, and operations were begun early in 1960. The facility covers fifty surface acres, impounds 1,500 acre feet of water, and cost $482,000.

If agriculture and cattle and water supplies all link the modern ranch to a long tradition, one other highly significant element in its recent history, the James Irvine Foundation, goes back, if not so far, at least to the 1930's and the second bearer of the name.[3] On February 24, 1937, more than ten years before his death, James Irvine drafted an indenture of trust creating a corporation, named "The

[3]The following section to the end of the indenture substantially reproduces a portion of the first edition of Cleland's *Irvine Ranch*.

James Irvine Foundation,'' to which he assigned fifty-one per cent of the stock of the Irvine Company. Myford Irvine was president of the foundation from its inception until his death; he was succeeded by N. Loyall McLaren.

After setting aside annually such sums from the income of the foundation as the trustees in their "sound discretion deem wise and expedient for investment" as an addition to the corpus of the trust, the trustees are to devote the remainder to the advancement "of any charitable use or purpose in the State of California as now is or may hereafter be authorized in the Articles of Incorporation of the Trustee [i.e., the foundation] and as the Board of Directors of the Trustee shall from time to time . . . select and determine." No part of the net income of the trust is to "inure to the benefit of any member of The James Irvine Foundation," nor may all of the income "be devoted to any one or two charities to the exclusion of others."

The carefully planned indenture contained these additional provisions:

. . . It is the purpose of said Trustor, by the creation of this trust and by vesting in the Trustee through its holding of said stock of The Irvine Company, the exercise of a controlling voice in the operation of its properties, to perpetuate the operation thereof and thus insure an adequate foundation for the charitable purposes herein provided. It is the Trustor's firm conviction that no other security could afford The James Irvine Foundation a more safe and stable investment than the capital stock of The Irvine Company, if this land holding is preserved and sustained at its present state of development, with such improvements, if any, as may be justified in the future. Portions of the land adjacent to and near the Pacific Coast and Newport Bay might from time to time be advantageously disposed of in various small parcels or units, and hill and unimproved property in larger units; but the great central valley acreage, together with such lands as are essential to the maintenance of the water supply thereto, should in the judgment of the Trustor, be held and operated as a unit. The Trustor also cautions against disbursement of too large a part of the income or surplus of The Irvine Company. In furtherance of the policy heretofore established, liberal reserves of income must be accumulated and held for future needs and against unforeseen contingencies which have never yet failed to recur.

... The Trustor interprets the charitable purposes of The James Irvine Foundation as stated in its Articles of Incorporation to include financial aid generally to worthy individuals, who through illness or misfortune are temporarily in need. There is, for example, a very large body of self-respecting citizens who are not wealthy enough to afford for their families and themselves that same high quality of medical and surgical and hospital care which is open to the wealthy and also the very poor. It is the desire and hope of the Trustor that The James Irvine Foundation may find a means of extending such temporary aid to as many as possible of these worthy individuals and families, and in so doing, that worthy citizens and families residing in Orange County, California, be not overlooked.

The Trustor also suggests that a revolving fund be created for loans not to exceed in the aggregate One Thousand ($1,000.00) Dollars per person, with very moderate rates of interest, to worthy students and scholars who are in need of financial aid to carry on their studies in institutions of learning in California, and also in moderate amounts to scientists or individuals engaged in research work who require financial assistance therein.

It is also the direction of the Trustor that charities receiving the substantial part of their support from taxation should not be beneficiaries of any of the property derived from this trust, but that all such property, available from time to time for the benefit of charities, shall be used for such charities as do not enjoy any substantial support through taxation.

In fulfilling its obligations under this trust, the foundation has quietly and without publicity granted major sums for capital improvements to almost every private university within the state of California and to a large number of hospitals in the Orange County and San Francisco Bay regions. The foundation works simply; its board is divided into two committees, one for northern, the other for southern California. Each committee submits its most worthy applications to semiannual meetings of the entire board, and the awards are granted commensurate with the funds available. Perhaps by these grants the Irvine name will engender its most precious light and warmth.

In addition to its educational and humanitarian responsibilities, the foundation exercises a controlling interest in the company itself, and here its position has been severely tested. An unusual controversy developed within the company, dating from 1957 when Joan Irvine Burt became a member of the board of directors. Mrs. Burt was the only child of James Irvine, III, who had predeceased his father in 1935. Since Mrs. Burt's accession to the board she has frequently been at odds with the other directors, including those who also represented the foundation's interests. She engaged in a series of attacks and charges to which the southern California press devoted considerable space.

Myford Irvine died on January 11, 1959. The directors elected as new president of the company Arthur J. Mc-Fadden, rancher, long-time business associate and loyal friend of the Irvines, and trustee of the foundation since its inception; and as vice-president, N. Loyall McLaren, business adviser to the second James Irvine and also an original trustee of the foundation. In the ensuing period, just short of two years, while McFadden served as chief executive of the company, many important undertakings, such as the Rattlesnake Canyon Dam and the Collins Radio Company lease, were consummated.

On entering office, both McFadden and McLaren held that their most immediate task would be the search for a younger man to serve as the company's president. A consulting firm was hired to conduct an extensive survey by interviewing leaders in business and banking, from New York to Los Angeles. The result, slightly more than a year after Myford Irvine's death, was a list of fifteen candidates.

The chief concern of McFadden's successor would be to operate the company efficiently and diplomatically, and from these standpoints, as well as others, the final choice, Charles Sparks Thomas, showed great insight. His previous experiences—as special assistant to Navy Secretary James Forrestal, as Under Secretary of the Navy, as Assistant Secretary of Defense, and finally as Secretary of the Navy—all proved his ability at handling difficult situations. In the Pentagon his quiet smile had witnessed transitions from steam to nuclear-powered ships, from propellers to jets, from subsonic to supersonic planes, and from gunpowder to missiles.

He had resigned as Secretary of the Navy at the end of three years (March 27, 1957) and, after a short interim, had accepted the invitation of Howard Hughes to become president of Trans World Airlines. Reorganized from top to bottom, TWA under his direction, after four years of losses, rose to one of the highest levels of profit in the industry. This was achieved, he says, "with people and their proper organization."

Thomas had known the Irvine Ranch since World War I when he flew the mail for the Navy between San Diego and San Pedro, looking down day after day on the ranch's bays, tidal basins, agricultural plains, and creased ridges. In the 1930's he was a member of a gun club which shot ducks in

Irvine sloughs and marshes. From above and below he knew the ranch as well as a mid-town New Yorker might know Central Park. It is not surprising that when Thomas was offered the Irvine job, the fruit was tempting. In October 1960 Charles Thomas became the fifth president of the Irvine Company.

Even if the Thomas administration proves as long and eventful as those of the first three Irvines, it will probably be remembered as the period of reorganization and projection. It became apparent that earlier planning, dating from 1946 in the coastal area of the ranch, required expansion to meet the changing times. It is not surprising that planning for the ranch has become a full-fledged department, involving specialists and the conversion of the old Irvine family ranch house into a maze of maps and molded projections. What is going on in the homestead today has little relevance to the long succession of engineers' reports and topographic charts which have left in the ranch offices a honeycomb vault containing no fewer than 2,000 maps and elevations. The newer approach, dating at least from 1959, can more accurately be called creative land-use planning, and the face of the future upon which it focuses is indeed complicated.

For example, the ranch, constant victim of the needs of burgeoning cities, school systems, and public utilities, has for many years been following the policy of placing monies received from condemnation in a replacement fund which is used to buy land elsewhere. Thus the directors have expanded their Flying D Ranch in Montana to cover 81,365 acres of deeded land (close to the present size of the parent ranch) plus leased land from the government which brings the total to near 92,000 acres. On the Montana ranch 5,700 grown cattle can be pastured, a capacity far exceeding that of the Orange County land. Likewise in the Imperial Valley the original acquisition of 2,400 acres in 1953 was augmented by continuance of the aforementioned policy until by the end of 1958 the Irvine Company owned 8,700 acres, and by 1961 it owned 11,150 acres in that important agricultural area. These are in some seven major sections, not contiguous as in Montana. The growth of these outlander ranches can certainly be called planning, and it has been going on for a long time. It envisions in a distant future, if not transplanting, at least expanding the Irvine agricultural tradition to the warm, desert valleys of Imperial County and the cattle-raising aspects to the Flying D, which Myford Irvine once called "the finest cattle ranch in Montana."

But meanwhile the immediate planning problem—one which inevitably leads far from the agricultural tradition—has been the orderly urbanization of the great original Orange County property, still in 1961 spreading across 88,256 acres. Much of the development of the 1950's went on without benefit of a paper-and-clay delineation; planning meant simply the accumulated foresight and experience of a few men. During the eleven years of Myford Irvine's administration and the two years of Arthur McFadden's, the ranch caused to be subdivided a good many key areas around Newport Bay and along the coast—Irvine Terrace, Westcliff, Harbor Highlands, Baycrest, Cameo Shores, Cameo Highlands, Irvine Cove, Harbor View Hills. The championship golf course of the Irvine Coast Country Club was completed. The Ford Motor Company (Aeronutronic Division) and the Collins Radio Company both leased large chunks of land and built important research plants. Even though these real-estate developments covered altogether approximately 1,100 acres, in aggregate their total area is relatively small compared with the magnitude of the planning to come.

The more serious, long-range urbanization of the ranch is associated with the architect William L. Pereira, who was retained as a consultant in connection with land acquisition for the University of California. Together with Charles Luckman, his partner at that time, he had been commissioned by the regents of the university in 1957 to study prospective sites for two new campuses in southern California. Their staff conducted four months of research, reading John Henry Newman on the meaning of a university, George Pierson on Yale, Samuel E. Morison on Harvard, and a host of volumes on Paris, Bologna, Glasgow, and higher education back to ancient Greece. They sought to discover what made a great university and what elements of a site might contribute to such greatness. A faculty, they concluded, is the most important ingredient, but the great university must in addition have gifted students, be near a cosmopolitan urban center, and provide residence for students and faculty near or on the campus. The "nobility" of its site should be able "to create a contemplative mood, to stimulate thought, and to inspire invention" and should invoke a "sense of place" bound up with its history, traditions, and associations. Given these elements of greatness, the new campus should possess enough land to avoid future congestion and should settle in a sympathetic supporting community.

In the East Los Angeles–Orange County area, a large number of possibilities was first narrowed to twenty-one sites, which were then carefully considered, rated, and compared. Five locations were found to be of prime quality; one of these was a stretch of gently rolling San

Joaquin foothills on the ranch, just east of the north tip of Upper Newport Bay, the site eventually chosen by the regents.

In the study the need for master planning the development of surrounding areas had stood out like a beacon. The regents, with Arthur McFadden one of their members, remembering difficulties on other of their campuses, considered this factor more and more important, and the Irvine Company came to see it as vital also to its own interests and those of the surrounding communities.

In March 1959, the Regents of the University of California and President McFadden of the Irvine Company requested Pereira and his associates to study in detail the site offered on the Irvine Ranch. The initial phase, completed in October 1959, established economic feasibility and the possibility of a satisfactory campus complex. A second document, "Second Phase Report for a University-Community Development in Orange County," was adopted as a guide by the Irvine directors in June 1960. In this work Pereira's associates and the company's own planning department took 10,000 acres of raw land, with the proposed university campus like an uncut emerald in the midst, and created the plan for a university-oriented community to bear the name of Irvine.

The university campus will have "inclusion areas" interlocked with its central core. These three parcels, roughly 220 acres each, will provide residences for single and married students, apartments and single-family dwellings for faculty and staff, churches, schools, and convenience shopping areas. A fourth parcel will be the urban focus, the university town itself, intended to nurture the character of traditional college towns, like Princeton, "in intimate pedestrian scale." The hope was also to revitalize the basic meaning of a community, somewhat on the pattern of a colonial New England town with political and civic interests taking the place of religious ties.

Near the university town, a dredged marsh will form a lake meandering through a golf course and residential districts. Other low lands will be converted into open green belts, and a small neck of university property will thrust through one such park to establish contact with Upper Newport Bay. The plans can thus suggest shells racing upon a 2,000-meter rowing course across the bay. With a suitable balance between diverse light industries, varied research firms, expanded residential areas, and the necessary roads and utilities, the growth of the university community is projected by phases at least to 1980, when the 10,000 acres should sustain a population of more than 50,000, including 15,000 students.

If master planning is essential for one area such as the university complex, why not for the whole? Hence in 1960 the directors of the Irvine Company retained the firm of William L. Pereira and Associates to prepare a master plan for the entire ranch. The directors recognized that such planning should not be static, and therefore they specified a flexible guide coupled with provisions for continuous re-evaluation.

The Irvine Ranch, an area four times that of the whole city of San Francisco, stands in the path of active urbanization. Its western border is nipped by the bulging cities of Santa Ana, Tustin, Orange, Costa Mesa, and Newport Beach. Two population streams surge toward it, south from Los Angeles and north from San Diego. But it remains as yet largely unscathed.

In this situation the opportunities for the development of the ranch are in many respects unprecedented. Specifically, the market already exists. There is no need to create an artificial demand for the property. Perhaps encouragement for certain kinds of investment may be required—light industry, for example—but the men of the company, in fact, have no precipitate desire to sell; they prefer development under a long-range plan. Their love for Orange County, their appreciation of the productivity of the soil itself, minimizes similarities with real-estate subdivision, where sales must be pushed to realize short-term gains. Many an arid southern California acre has been rushed onto the market by creating artificial demand without any sound community interest; the possibility of avoiding that pattern is truly a great opportunity.

For ranch master-planning purposes the 88,256 acres were divided like a pagoda into three tiers. The lower story, the coastal section, covering about 35,000 acres from the sea to the northern boundaries of the planned university community, will absorb the first wave of urbanization. The central tier, some 20,000 acres of lush fields and orchards, will preserve the Irvine agricultural tradition, not only because of its soil and climate, but because the planners feel that the preservation of agriculture is essential to the economic health of southern California and, to a lesser extent, because the Marine jet planes streaking out from the El Toro Air Base disturb oranges less than they disturb human beings. The mountain section, 33,000 acres of rugged peaks and ragged canyons, well suited for recreation, will require considerable population pressure before urban development occurs.

The agricultural future of the ranch is of as much concern to the planners as any other part of the whole program. Agriculture, of course, plays a vital role in the economy. It not only provides food for exploding population while offering green, open-space relief from crowded metropolitan centers, but it also produces important tax revenues far exceeding the cost of services it requires, needing no sewers, utilities, police protection, or schools. With the great urban push into the county have come subsequent tax needs, and authorities are pressured to assess open lands with an eye toward their future urban use, rather than their present agricultural use. Should such tax assessment tendencies continue, there can be only a precarious future for agriculture on the Irvine Ranch. Should large areas have to be liquidated owing to these tax pressures on agricultural lands, the common pattern of southern California's haphazard development would occur on Irvine property.

In 1964 the Irvine Ranch will celebrate the centenary of the first Irvine-Bixby-Flint purchase of land. A hundred years after that purchase it is possible to ride across the domain from northeast to southwest and feel that every period of southern California history still lives upon it. First comes a mountainous wilderness of deer and coyote and quail, hot and dry, pungent with sage, pocked with cactus clumps. Serra and Portolá would recognize it immediately. Southward are cattle roaming the gentle hills, the land of Figueroa and Sepúlveda, "of the large and charitable air." Farther is the magic green of irrigated agriculture, including vast acres where the meadowlark greets a lonely sunrise as he has for rancher and small farmer since the middle of the nineteenth century. And, finally, nearing the coast, stretches an urban complex of recreational living which the twentieth century catalyzed in southern California. With the annual spring roundup as one face of the past and with the planned community as one facet of the future, the ranch, as it approaches its centennial, continues to keep a multilevel rendezvous with history. Its long rural traditions will inevitably bind it for decades to come; but the impact of change is already felt on the land.

INDEX

INDEX

tration of ranch, 98, 101-102, 103,
104, 105-107, 111, 112, 114-115,
117-118, 121, 123, 125, 133, 134;
marriage and family, 100, 101, 110,
137 and *n*; donations to the community, 104, 135; outside enterprises, 111, 116, 118, 120, 125; interest in scientific experiments,
126, 127; death, 136-137; incorpo-
ration of James Irvine Foundation,
144-145
Irvine, James, III (1893-1935), 101,
137 and *n*, 147
Irvine, James Myford, 137*n*
Irvine, Joan. *See* Burt, Joan Irvine
Irvine, John, 61
Irvine, Kathryn Brown, 137*n*
Irvine, Kathryn Helena. *See* Lillard,
Kathryn Helena Irvine
Irvine, Linda Jane. *See* Gaede, Linda
Jane Irvine
Irvine, Margaret Byrne, 87-88, 89
Irvine, Myford, 101, 137-138, 145,
147, 148, 150
Irvine, Nettie Rice, 60, 65-66, 87*n*
Irvine, William, 59, 60
Irvine, Calif., 132, 152
Irvine, Harker & Co., 60
"Irvine & Co.," 60
Irvine Beach and Country Club Es-
tates, 133*n*
Irvine Bowl, 135
Irvine Citrus Association, 124
Irvine Coast Country Club, 150
Irvine Company: directors and offi-
cers of, 79*n*, 81*n*, 137, 147, 148,
149; real-estate sales, leases, and
subdivisions, 85, 108-109, 108*n*,
116-117, 119, 122*n*, 132-135, 133*n*,
145, 150-151; incorporated, 101,
115; agricultural practices of, 102-
103, 119, 120, 124; and water conservation program, 121-122, 122*n*;
salt plant, 126; stock of, 145-146;
master planning, 149-155
Irvine Cove, 150
Irvine Foundation. *See* James Irvine
Foundation
Irvine Lake (Santiago Reservoir),
122 and *n*, 123, 144

Irvine Park (sometimes called
"County Park"), 21, 84, 104
Irvine Ranch, 5, 21, 56, 59, 66, 80, 82,
120, 126, 135, 136, 148, 149; location described, 4, 67, 69-70; ante-
cedent land grants, 8, 16, 20, 25,
38; land owned by Irvine-Flint-
Bixby, 43, 67, 75; cattle and sheep,
67, 68, 73, 75, 95, 103-104, 107, 110,
124, 139, 140, 142-143, 150; ranch
problems, 72-74, 103, 109-110;
wages, 73-74, 107; tenant farming,
75, 96, 102-103, 107, 109, 113, 140;
and the railroads, 75-77, 92-94;
land-title challenges, 75-77, 94, 128;
Irvine acquires full interest in, 77,
78; sales and leases, 79, 89-92, 108-
109, 132-134, 150-151; rights of
way, 81, 92-94, 98-99, 110, 125, 132,
134-135; inheritance and appraisal,
87-89, 101; field crops, 96, 101, 104-
105, 107, 110-111, 113, 124, 140,
141*n*; tree crops, 96, 104, 105, 107,
116, 124, 140, 141-142, 141*n*; natural disasters, 97, 103-104, 117-119;
water supply, 104, 117, 120-123,
143-144; mineral products, 124-
126; future plans, 138, 140, 152-155
Irvine Terrace, 150
Irvine Valencia Growers Association, 124

James Irvine Foundation, 79*n*, 144-
147
Jimeno Casarín, Manuel, 14-15
Johnson, Santiago, 23
Jones, Otis, 134

Kalisher, Wolf, 42
Koll, Frederick W., 35
Krauss, C. F., 108, 118
Kroeber, Alfred L., 5

Laguna, Calif. *See* Laguna Beach,
Calif.
Laguna Art Festival, 135
Laguna Beach, Calif., 4, 20, 108, 132,
134-135

Vejar, Juan C., 14
Ventura County, 102, 113, 114, 119
Verdugo, José María, 7
Vigilance Committee of 1856, 65n

Walnut Acres, 120
Walnuts, 96, 104, 107, 117, 124, 141n, 142
Warner, J. J., 24, 31, 37
Waterman, Robert W., 91
Water supply: local sources, 34, 44, 79, 82, 104, 117, 119, 120-122, 134-135, 143-144, 146; Metropolitan Water District, 122-123, 133n, 135, 144
Westcliff, 150
West Shore Oil Company, 125n
West Virginia, 101
Wheat, 140
Wheeler, Kathryn Anita Lillard, 137n
Whidden, George, 91, 95, 96, 97-98
White, Stephen M., 89
Whiting, Dwight, 94
Wilmington harbor, 72
Wolfskill, William, 35, 36, 41-42, 44-45
Wool, 57, 58, 68, 70, 72, 95, 143
Work, Hubert, 76
World War II, 132

Ybarra, José Desiderio, 31-32
Yorba, Bernardo, 19, 25, 31, 34
Yorba, Domingo, 33
Yorba, Guadalupe, 17
Yorba, Inocencia Reyes de, 44
Yorba, Isabel, 33
Yorba, José Antonio (d. 1825), 12-13, 16, 31-32
Yorba, José Antonio, Jr. (son of José Antonio Yorba, d. 1825), 13-15
Yorba, José Antonio (son of Tomás Yorba), 17
Yorba, Josefa, 17
Yorba, Josefa Grijalva de, 16
Yorba, José Ramón, 34
Yorba, Juan, 17
Yorba, María. See Burruel, María Yorba de
Yorba, Presentación. See Serrano, Presentación Yorba de
Yorba, Ramón, 31, 33
Yorba, Ramona, 17
Yorba, Susana, 33
Yorba, Teodosio, 25-26, 31, 33, 34, 44, 47, 75, 76
Yorba, Tomás Antonio, 12, 15-18, 22, 34
Yorba, Vicenta Sepúlveda de, 17
Yorba family, 15, 18-19, 24, 26, 31-32, 36, 79